FORGIVENESS & DIVORCE

A Step-by-Step Guide using The 15-Minute Rule

Caroline Buchanan

DARK RIVER

TABLE OF CONTENTS

INTRODUCTION

It's a sad but inevitable fact that divorce is accompanied by pain. Sometimes, awful pain that you fear you might never recover from.

But if you could forgive anyone, or everyone (including yourself) who has caused you real heartache – leaving you happy, joyous and free to live your life to the absolute full – what would you say?

Yes please?

Bring it on?

Well, you're in the right place, because – I promise you – I can enable you to do just that.

Even if you are one of the lucky ones who finds forgiving others relatively easy, divorce is something that will truly test you. More likely than not, it will trigger all kinds of unresolved issues from your childhood, that can leave you feeling completely overwhelmed. Not only are you going through the agonies of separation and divorce from your spouse, but also unhealed wounds from your early life can burst open again.

Crisis, however, is an opportunity to grow…And one of the best ways to do that is to embrace the option of forgiveness.

For many, the lack of forgiveness can be – and often is – a destructive, dominating, and debilitating force. Many people literally crumple up through lack of forgiveness. They eat themselves up, constantly chastise themselves, harm other people, and harm themselves.

Unforgiveness (not being able to forgive) can actually make us ill, or contribute to maladies. According to CBN, 'Of all cancer patients, 61% have forgiveness issues and of those more than half are severe. The first step in forgiveness therapy is recognising forgiveness is not the same thing as condoning what a person did, which is the major hurdle for most patients.'

Cancer surgeon Dr. Steven Standiford says unforgiveness makes people sick and keeps them sick.

'It's important to treat emotional wounds or disorders because they really can hinder someone's reactions to the treatment, even someone's willingness to pursue treatment,' he says.

We know that love is what makes the world go round, and yet forgiveness, which is such a demonstration of love, is all too often ignored or denied. The ability to forgive – and accept forgiveness – is a very powerful enabler. And for those who master it, the rewards are wonderful.

This book will show you the following:

- How forgiveness will change your world dramatically
- How to find forgiveness no matter how impossible it seems
- How forgiving yourself will transform your life
- How to conquer the fallacy of fear
- How to shed the crippling baggage of anger and resentment
- How to dissolve the destructive power of guilt
- The game of Hide and Seek. How to banish the stifling power of shame
- How to choose your thoughts wisely
- How to create a life beyond your wildest dreams

All I ask is that you give the exercises a real go.

Don't just read the book, and pass over the tasks. It is the 'doing' that will transform your life, not just the reading!

Let's start!

\ Divorce isn't such a tragedy. A tragedy's staying in /
an unhappy marriage, teaching your children the
wrong things about love.
Nobody ever died of divorce.

Jennifer Weiner, Fly Away Home

CHAPTER ONE: FORGIVENESS WITH THE 15-MINUTE RULE

Congratulations. In opening this book, you have made a wise decision and opened the door to a much happier life.

You are about to get in touch with the life-changing force of forgiveness – the mindful, deliberate act of releasing your feelings of resentment or vengeance towards others (your spouse or former spouse, or maybe a friend who cheated with your partner, or anyone else at the heart of your divorce), irrespective of whether they actually deserve your clemency.

You do not have to condone appalling behaviours to forgive.

Forgiveness joyously obliterates bitterness, anger, hatred and frustration and enables positive and life-affirming gifts to grow in their place.

Perhaps you blame yourself – rightly or wrongly – for the breakdown of your relationship, so equally importantly, it is time to forgive yourself (something many people desperately need to do). The inability to forgive oneself is at the root of depression and chronic anxiety for many people.

This book centres around my 15-minute rule. In a nutshell, the 15-minute rule is a way to break down work into manageable intervals, separated by short breaks. It also shows you how new and constructive ways of thinking will make such a fabulous difference to your life. In working my tried and tested 15-minute rule, you will overcome a big problem far sooner than you might think possible.

So, what might 'forgiveness' mean for you?

Sit back, close your eyes, and paint a picture of just how wonderful it would be if you could drop that huge weight from your shoulders; that painful load that you have been carrying around for a long time. For those of you who feel an instant sense of peace at the very thought of being free from it all, then just imagine how your life would change if you could *really* and *truly* forgive or feel forgiven.

The bliss of forgiveness

Strangely enough, many people are not even aware that it is the forgiveness issue (or more accurately 'unforgiveness') that is causing them to be unhappy, depressed, or desperately stuck in an unhealthy groove following divorce. But, it so often is!

You may well know exactly what you're struggling with here, and are longing to be free of it; or perhaps thoughts are just beginning to filter through about your need to resolve some very unhelpful thinking styles.

The ability to forgive and accept forgiveness is a very powerful enabler. And for those who master it, the rewards are literally glorious.

Personally, I always thought I was pretty good at forgiving others, but I have been appalling at forgiving myself. You may feel exactly the same? Whether it's failing to forgive someone else you struggle with, or truly forgiving yourself, you are living your life in a way that is severely hampered. And it's not necessary. You are worth so much more than that.

There are all kinds of emotions tied up with unforgiveness. Fear, anger, control, criticism, resentment, jealousy and envy to name but a few. Read on, because I can promise you a much better life. Indeed, as Einstein said:

> There is no problem, there is only a solution.

Albert Einstein

When I got in touch with the power of forgiveness, my life was transformed. In fact, if you talk to anyone who has experienced it, life suddenly makes sense in a way it never did before. You feel more loving and giving than ever before (even if you were loving and giving in the first place, which of course you were!).

Over the course of this book, I will urge you to look deep inside and ask yourself how long this has been going on for you, and whether you've been consciously aware of it or not. If we are not facing our problems, we are depriving ourselves, our loved ones, and the world!

By justifying our actions, thoughts, and feelings, we are denying so much of our true selves. *In terms of a marriage breakdown, even if you never want to see the people again, they are still with you, living rent-free in your head!*

Remember that to forgive does not mean to condone something. It does not mean you think the behaviour was acceptable. *It is saying you don't want it to hurt you anymore.*

I'm sure you tell yourself from time to time that you have to find a way forward on the forgiveness issue but – odds on – procrastination is getting in the way. It's so easy to put stuff off, especially when it's painful. But every time you do that, you are adding weight to the problem. It's the snowball effect. Perhaps it feels just too big to make a start? But do you want to stay stuck in the problem, or do you want to live in the solution? It's a no-brainer really. Commit to the techniques in this book, and I will hold your hand and guide you all the way to forgiveness.

You are not alone.

With my tried, tested, and much-loved 15-Minute Rule, I can show you how to come out from the darkness and into the light. The sunny uplands are waiting for you. You really can live your life to the full from hereon in.

If you make a commitment to do it, I will guarantee you positive results.

'It works, if you work it' as they say in 12-step programmes!

CHAPTER TWO: HOW TO WORK THE 15-MINUTE RULE FOR FORGIVENESS

There is something very special and unique about the 15-minute time frame. It's not too long to be burdensome, yet it encourages your creativity and frees you from the horror of trying to get things perfect. (You can always tidy things up later.)

But the other special thing about it is that 15 minutes is long enough to achieve something worthwhile and valuable. AND WHAT'S MORE, YOU'VE STARTED! You've laid that vital foundation stone.

As I have discovered for myself, the higher you get up the mountain, the better the view!

So, now, it's time to begin your wonderful new life…

Time For Change

The start line

Task 1: Get Ready, Get Set

Prepare a new file on your laptop, or get together a notebook and pen. Then set an alarm for 15 minutes.

15 min

This first 15 minutes is about brainstorming the subject of Forgiveness. Write down anything that comes into your head that you think will help you; for example, your first thoughts when you consider the subject of forgiveness. 'Freedom from pain!' you might write. Or 'Tremendous relief'. You, after all, are your own expert.

Remember, nobody is looking over your shoulder so write, draw, whatever fits, with complete freedom.

Maybe you'll write 'Impossible to forgive!' or 'He/She doesn't deserve it' or 'How can I forgive myself for that?!' Other example entries in your notebook or on your computer might include: 'Forgiveness would be blissful!' or 'I could tackle anything if I could forgive; I will no longer be a slave to the past' or 'I could sleep at night!'

When your alarm goes off, STOP IMMEDIATELY, even if you're desperate to carry on writing and exploring. You need to give yourself the message you can trust yourself. You need to trust in the boundary you have created. *This is very important.* If you are disciplined with this time frame, it will keep you focused, motivated, and keen to try it again.

You won't dread coming back to the task either, because you know it's a safe and secure place to be.

Remember this – self-discipline is actually being kind to yourself. And being kind to yourself is a rare thing for some people.

I suggest you do your first three sessions within a 72-hour period. There is no need to procrastinate on finding that time over three days. You can always grab 15 minutes over the busiest of times. Especially as it will be such an investment in your future.

One of the Rule's strongest points is it can be used for any task, no matter how overwhelming, because virtually anything is manageable for 15 minutes. Remember that too.

Dreading a task is a nightmare that just won't go away. Facing your fear and getting on and doing it leaves you feeling wonderful. The feeling of achievement with something so positive is palpable.

Task 2: Go Forward with Forgiveness

Set your alarm for another 15 minutes, no more, no less. Is it forgiving others or forgiving yourself that's the problem? It might well (of course) be both, in which case head up one document 'Forgiving Others' and another named 'Forgiving Myself'.

Write down all the feelings you associate with the underlying problem(s) and any ideas you might have about positive solutions.

STOP when the alarm goes off. You might be in a frenzy to carry on writing or, conversely, you might feel stuck. Wherever you are on this, it's time for a break. Even if it's just for 15 minutes! Remember, you are learning to trust your boundaries.

Task 3: Follow the Path

Carry on from where you left off. As this will be your third session, you can stop after 15 minutes, or you can carry on for as long as you like. However, STOP the minute you get bored, tired, or fed up.

Write down any further insights you've had in 'Forgiving Others' and 'Forgiving Myself' and then visualise what forgiveness in both documents would mean to you. Imagine how you would feel if all is forgiven. Get in touch with that incredible feeling of release and freedom. You will start to know that if you can do this, you can achieve anything. Begin to acknowledge the sensation of relief and the beginnings of recovery.

The 15-Minute Rule is not just about contained, focused time frames. It brings with it a huge feeling of safety, and you won't know just how much until you try it. Once you start working the Rule, you will be amazed at the many extraordinary benefits. They are way out of proportion to the simple idea and the small commitment of time. You will be keen to carry on because the results very soon prove to you that your life is now undergoing amazing changes.

Now have you done that work yet? You could commit to doing Task 1, shortly followed by Tasks 2 and 3, before you read any further. Or if you'd prefer to read the whole book first, and then do the tasks afterwards; then, of course, that's entirely up to you.

Task 4: Reward Yourself

15 min Virtue is its own reward, but that doesn't stop you giving yourself a treat when you've done a piece of work. Snuggle up to someone, be it a person or a pet. Give yourself a hug and a pat on the back if you're on your own. In fact, do that anyway! You could reward yourself with a favourite television programme, a good read, a hot or cold drink or a tasty snack (probably best to make it a healthy one, because you are now on the road to taking good care of yourself!).

Also, try to remember that when you've had more than a day's break from your forgiveness project, go back to just 15 minute periods of work for your next two sessions. Again, from the third 15-minute session, carry on as long as you like, but STOP the minute you get bored, tired, or fed up.

Cuppa tea time!

Healing Power

I use my 15-Minute Rule every day of my life. I recommend it highly because it puts constructive thought into action – and fast.

Whilst most people reading this book will be going through their own divorces, here is a short story about forgiveness and divorce from a slightly different perspective. It is included to show how the 15-Minute Rule can work no matter what the circumstance. This is Carla's story.

'My parents divorced when I was four years old, and my upbringing was certainly dysfunctional. My father seemed to be permanently angry and my mother tiptoed around on eggshells trying to keep him from losing his temper.

'I was the youngest of three sisters and our parents' examples didn't do any of us much good. I married a man just like my father and needless to say it didn't last. I had counselling afterwards which helped me to understand a lot, but I still felt angry with my parents and kept them at a distance.

'I started doing the 15-Minute Rule for Forgiveness a few months ago, and it really did open my eyes to all sorts of stuff that I had never thought about before. I saw things in a different way. I acknowledged I was *still* angry with my parents and instead of stuffing that anger down as usual, I followed Caroline's suggestions and thankfully found a constructive way of working it through. Basically, I allowed myself to then feel the anger, without censoring myself, and kept reassuring myself that I wouldn't act out on it. I would acknowledge it, deal with it, and look forward to healing from it

'It took a bit of work but I have now forgiven my parents! I am amazed at how much lighter I feel and how this has a knock-on positive effect in all areas of my life.'

So, now you know the basics of the 15-Minute Rule for Forgiveness, and its truly positive effects. What's more, you have the beginnings of your toolkit. The structure is up and running, and you are on the path to peace of mind.

Remember the following:

I am not what happened to me – I am
what I choose to become.

Carl Jung

CHAPTER THREE: THE FALLACY OF FEAR

Are you feeling a tad excited now that you're on the brink of enormous change? Or are you fearful? Life after a divorce will bring lots of new opportunities, rekindle some old ones, but – no matter what – it will bring change; to some the very word 'change', let alone the deed, can be scary. But we need to get out of our (dis)comfort zone to smell the roses. While fear is natural and sometimes very helpful to us, more often than not it is imaginary.

A lovely acronym for fear is False Evidence Appearing Real, and it can drive us crazy. Work the 15-Minute Rule on this, and you will come to understand so much more about yourself. Then just watch your fear levels drop dramatically.

Task 5: What Frightens You About Forgiveness?

Again, get out your Forgiveness work, set the timer on your clock or your phone for 15 minutes, and write down the following question. *Forgiveness, what is it that frightens me about the idea?*

Now answer...

You will undoubtedly find fear in your reluctance to forgive.

- 'If I forgive him, will he think I'm stupid?'
- 'If I forgive her, will she hurt me again?'
- 'Is it wrong to forgive myself?'
- 'Maybe I don't deserve forgiveness?'

As you write down your fears, you will naturally challenge some of them that might seem a bit silly. Be gentle with yourself. Whatever anxiety comes up, honour it and use your Adult self to reassure the frightened Child within you (more about this, below).

Work the 15-Minute Rule in the way I've suggested until you've listed all your fears, and then start to examine them. For example, fearing you'll be thought stupid or a pushover – if you forgive – can be looked at from many angles. Let's say a woman is frightened her unfaithful partner will think she's crackers if she forgives his infidelity. Will she effectively be absolving him of responsibility for the breakdown of the relationship? If she has her negative hat on, she could persuade herself that he will indeed think she's a pushover (and that he'll walk away from the marriage without being suitably contrite). However, if she is thinking positively, she will know it's what she *thinks of herself* that matters, not what the other person thinks of her. Now, if she thinks she's being a pushover, and makes the decision to change that or accept it, she's in a much stronger position, either way.

'Knowing what must be done does away with fear,' is a quote by civil rights activist Rosa Parks. Very true.

The Power of Transactional Analysis

I don't know whether or not you're familiar with Transactional Analysis but it is a very helpful tool to have in your kit. For those who know about it, I remind you to use it on a regular basis. For those who don't, Transactional Analysis (TA) is a psychoanalytic theory, which suggests we have – within each of us – an Adult Self, a Parent Self, and a Child Self.

Eric Berne, the originator of TA, basically says our three ego states, Parent, Adult and Child, are the way we experience the world.

- The Parent self can behave in two ways - the Nurturing, Loving parent, and the Critical, Controlling parent.
- The Adult self knows how to think and behave as a grown-up.
- The Child self can take on three different roles.
  - The Natural Child, who is honest and vulnerable and loves to play and have fun.
  - The Little Professor who enjoys exploring and trying new things. These two combined make up what is known as the Free Child.
  - Finally, there is the Adaptive Child who has done just that – adapted to cope with their lot by finding a way to fit in with their family or fight against their circumstances.

The Parent, Adult, and Child who reside within us can, and do, have all sorts of internal conversations from their various standpoints. But, of course, we also play these roles with Other People. Obviously, there are many combinations in the way we behave in our relationships.

Our Adult state is the only one that is not directly connected to our past and is often where we feel most comfortable.

Grown-ups, generally speaking, are best off communicating with each other using their Adult selves. But all too often we can slip into other ways of relating. We can get into a parent/child dynamic with someone else and if it's you being a nurturing parent, and you're looking after someone who needs a bit of mothering or fathering, then that's you being kind and loving.

As adults, when we're fearful, we are very often in our Child self. This is where many of our 'What ifs' come from that can terrorise us at times. What if he turns my children against me? What if I have a breakdown? What if I never find love again? What if I completely run out of money? What if I can't cope when my mother dies? What if I'm terminally ill?

If we're fearful about *forgiveness* the 'What ifs' might say If I forgive him/her will it be dangerous?; What if I lose my self-esteem, what if I lose myself in the process?; Or, when it comes to forgiving ourselves, the fear could be there will be some form of punishment. What if I have an accident? What if the release from self-torture sends me crazy? What if I make a real failure of my life? What if it becomes possible to achieve all my goals?

Many people are frightened of their potential for huge success!

If just reading this gives you the shivers, be assured that I will be offering you solutions to anything, but anything, that is freaking you out. How can I do that? Because I've been there. Literally. I've looked at forgiveness from many angles and realised, only very recently, that the child within me had been running the show; dominating my attitude towards forgiveness (and self-forgiveness).

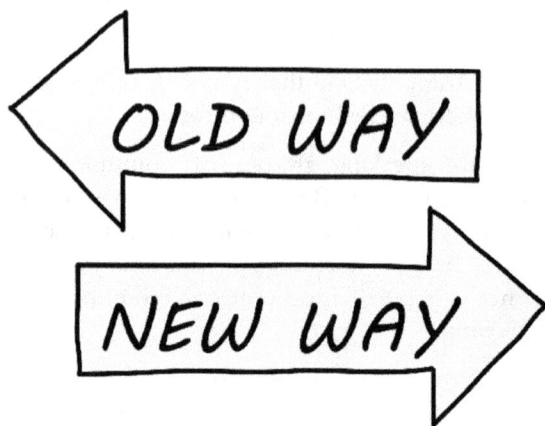

Thoughts of adapt or perish

Face to Face with Fear

When we face our fears (and forgiveness is a big fear for many people)
our world opens up dramatically. Of course, the biological roots of
fear are there to protect us from danger, to encourage the fight or
flight response. Faced with an angry tiger, we have to make a quick
decision. But so many of our fears are hangovers from the past and
have no relevance now. As I've said before, that which we fear – e.g.,
abandonment – has already happened. And we're still here – we lived
to tell the tale. Once we have taken constructive action about our fear,
not only is it a waste of time to keep reliving it, but it also does us
damage. It hurts us, and we're now in the business of healing.

'Fear dominated my life,' says Evie. 'But when I analysed it, I realised
that the permanent terror of being rejected really did belong to my
childhood, and not my adult life. Looking at that head on has made a
big difference. I've begun to know that I'm safe now.'

CHAPTER FOUR: FORGIVING OTHERS OR FORGIVING YOURSELF?

So which of Forgiving others or Forgiving yourself is your problem? You may well struggle with both. Either way, it is causing you major problems, some of which you may be unaware of at the moment.

Task 6: Start Your List [Forgiving Others]

Time now to concentrate on one of your two documents. Let's start with *Forgiving Others*. Use the 15-Minute Rule to think about and record all your thoughts on the subject. I promise you, it won't be overwhelming if you use the Rule. It's a really safe timeframe to explore your feelings.

15 min

List everyone involved in the divorce – or indeed your life – that you struggle to forgive. Whether it's many or few, let's think about what the idea of forgiveness means to you. List the reasons why you would like to forgive, and then list the reasons why you don't want to. Then, using the 15-Minute Rule in any way that suits you, let's explore together the reasons why you might not have conquered this mountain; the mountain that has been obscuring your view.

Possible Reasons not to Forgive Others

- The person doesn't deserve it
- Why should I forgive?
- I can't condone their unacceptable behaviour
- Fear of surrendering myself
- Fear of belittling myself
- Fear of loss of my identity
- Fear of change
- Fear of being free

Now continue listing any other fears you may have.

No matter what has happened to you, no matter how awful, you have the power to forgive. Parents of murdered children have managed it. People who have been horrendously damaged have managed it. Imagine the worst possible scenario and be assured that someone, somewhere, has been able to forgive just that. Impossible you say? No, it's not. It really is true that what doesn't kill us makes us stronger.

On the other extreme, those who seek revenge for the atrocities they've suffered will get nothing worthwhile whatsoever. All they will find is more grief.

Now we might fantasise about getting revenge, knowing we would never act on it. And while imagining getting our own back is natural, and may bring momentary relief, we would be much better off spending our energy on the idea of forgiveness. Of course, we're 'allowed' to feel angry about what's happened and to acknowledge how upset we are. It's very important to do so. **Feel**, **Deal**, and **Heal** is a phrase that can be very helpful.

'There is no healing without feeling' is something I heard the other day. By allowing the feelings to present themselves – experiencing them instead of running away from them – we can deal with the feelings by accepting them, and then think of constructive ways of letting them go. A wonderful therapist I once had, encouraged me to think of accepting painful thoughts as passing clouds, before putting them on a train, watching the doors close, and watching the train move away.

If we've been hurt by someone in a major way, or a minor way, we always have the choice on how to deal with the hurt constructively.

Although this does not relate to marriage, it involves the end of two relationships. Back in time, I once had a so-called friend. We were sharing a flat in our twenties and I came home unexpectedly one day to find my boyfriend at the time wearing nothing but his underpants. He didn't have a key. 'She let me in because I happened to be passing, was tired, and needed a sleep in your bed,' he said.

Looking back, I dealt with it amazingly well! As he was about the fifth boyfriend she'd taken a pop at, I thought it was time to move out. What's more, I have long since forgiven her and have compassion for her today. However, when she resurfaced decades on (I literally bumped into her), I politely refused the offer of resuming our friendship. I didn't want to invite more fear into my life especially as she never apologised. 'We had such fun!' she said. 'We must get together again.' Hmmm.

The above was relatively small fry for me because I had much bigger issues that needed forgiveness.

Some I didn't even acknowledge for years. Family stuff that was incredibly painful. Just like divorce, we can get so used to bad stuff so that, of course, it feels 'normal' for us at the time. But not anymore. We really don't have to adapt to what's really not right for us.

Above all things – *to thine own self be true* and all that!

Task 7: Focus on the Favours of Forgiveness

Let's concentrate on the reasons why you *should* forgive people. List them within a 15-minute time frame and try to provide detail if you can. For example, 'My anger and resentment towards my ex-husband sets a bad example to my son. By forgiving my husband, I will stop undermining the relationship between my son and his father; a relationship which is very important in these formative years.'

15 min

Forgiveness brings so many rewards to you and everyone around you.

Reasons to Forgive

- To stop driving yourself mad
- Peace of mind
- Better mental, spiritual, and physical health
- The right thing to do for you and everyone around you
- Serenity
- Shed a weight that's been hideous to carry
- Stop being so stuck
- Freedom from the pain
- Ability to move on
- A gigantic step in the right direction
- A small step for you, a leap (or giant one) for mankind
- Major growth
- A much richer self
- Enlightenment

- A good example to everyone around you

Add anything else that comes to mind for you – and share it around so others can benefit from your wisdom!

Task 8: What Would You Say to Your Best Friend?

Spend 15 minutes recording or writing down what you would say to a loved one who was having real trouble forgiving someone who had been harmed in the same way as you. It will be a real eye-opener...

15 min

Once you've written it, savour it and digest. It might read something like this: 'Of course you feel so hurt and angry at the way Frank humiliated you in front of everyone. When Gary did it to me, I told him to get stuffed, as you know. But I'm really glad I forgave him because the resentment was eating me away. Once I felt calmer, I accepted his apology, and I'm very glad I did. You know what he's like. With Frank, we need to work out a plan on how best to deal with him in the future! What I found really helpful was when I mentally decided to give Gary's madness back to him, rather than taking it on board myself. It doesn't belong to me, thank goodness.'

Forgiving Yourself

Now comes the time to start work on your *Forgiving Yourself* document. Are you sitting comfortably?

So many of us relate to not feeling good enough, so much so that I think sometimes it might simply be part of the human condition. A lot of it (as I said earlier) will have roots in our childhood. Even if you had a fabulously loving and secure background, with ideal parents or carers, you will have experienced some very unpleasant things along the way.

But for the many of us who had upbringings with more difficulties than a hiccough or two, we didn't grow up having all our basic childhood needs met. Children often blame themselves when something goes wrong and this is a heart-breaking fact of life that could actually be changed for the better if every parent was aware of it.

If they're not resolved at the time, these sentiments and perceptions *get carried through* into adult life.

When you come from a place that has led you to blame yourself for everything, a childhood which adapted you to feeling overly responsible, you will no doubt find it very difficult to forgive yourself, and sadly you have probably been identifying with the following:

Perceived Reasons not to Forgive Yourself

- I don't deserve it
- Why should I forgive myself?
- I'm a bad person
- I can't condone my unacceptable behaviour
- Fear of surrendering myself to the unknown
- Who am I without guilt?
- I might combust if I let go of my guilt and shame
- Freedom feels very scary

Now, in your own document, add all the other thoughts you beat yourself up with.

Task 9: Become Your Own Agony Aunt

15 min

Before I go any further, what would you say to someone who came to you confessing exactly the same thing you can't forgive yourself for? Write down or record *exactly* what you would say. Read, or listen to it, again. And again.

I bet you a zillion pounds you haven't been nearly as hard on them as you have been on yourself. In fact, you've probably been quite loving to them, if not *very* loving!

Are you feeling some compassion for yourself now? There hasn't been nearly enough of that around before now, has there? I had bucket loads of compassion for other people, but virtually none for myself. These days, I can find some.

Task 10: Think and Think Again

Spend time processing your thoughts on how harsh you have been on yourself – and how you wouldn't treat anyone else like that! Now, write down how you're going to do it differently in the future.

Let's walk together to try to find more compassion for YOU. Here's a brief list to get you started on the right road.

Reasons to Forgive Yourself

- To stop driving yourself mad
- Peace of mind
- Better mental, spiritual and physical health
- The right thing to do
- Serenity
- Shed a weight that's been hideous to carry
- Stop being so stuck
- Freedom from the pain
- Ability to move on
- A gigantic step in the right direction
- A small step for you, a leap (or giant one) for mankind
- Major growth
- A much richer self
- Enlightenment
- A good example to everyone around you

The list above contains the *same*(!) reasons, then, that would apply to forgiving someone else…

Are you feeling things shifting a bit now? Are you beginning to see the light? I hope so, but if you were anything like me – every time I saw a glimmer, I'd soon snuff it out again. I would see a flicker of hope for self-forgiveness – and then I would beat myself up. Overwhelmed by feelings that I didn't deserve it.

NB: We do deserve it!

You can take comfort now that the seeds of forgiveness are well and truly planted.

We can so easily hurt ourselves because we feel bad. That, in itself, can become a powerful addiction. You may have made a decision that what you did was bad and so you continue to punish yourself, no matter what anyone else says. Time now to change this – please.

I'm sure you're familiar with the 'Do as you would be done by' concept? Well, let's turn that one on its head for a minute and try 'Do for yourself what you would do for others.'

CHAPTER FIVE: THE CRIPPLING BAGGAGE OF ANGER AND RESENTMENT

This forgiveness stuff is all very well for someone else, you might be thinking, but surely it cannot be this simple? Do you feel it's different for you? You cannot possibly forgive that person for what they did and/or you can't ever forgive yourself for what you did – or didn't do.

You're very angry with yourself – or A. N. Other.

Let's look at it another way. Anger and resentment, expressed or not, hampers us in a way we might not fully understand. If we lose our temper, do we analyse exactly what happened? Do we take responsibility for our behaviour, no matter what the other person has said or done? If not, how can we possibly stop doing something that leaves us feeling awful time and time again? Or do we bury our anger and resentment, stuffing it all down because it's too scary or uncomfortable to tackle? The thing is… all that energy could be put to much better use.

It's helpful for us to reflect on the following quotation:

'Resentment is like swallowing poison and expecting the other person to die.'

It suddenly dawned on me a few years ago that many people fall into the category of blaming other people for everything (blamers), or conversely, blaming only themselves. I call them blamees. Sometimes people switch from one position to the other, before settling into the place that feels like home.

Of course, there are the healthy folk – the enviable ones we all aspire to be – who take full responsibility for their mistakes but don't take on everyone else's, to boot. The question here is – how do we get there?

The following might help you to see if you are a blamer or a blamee (if you don't know).

You discover your partner has cheated on you with a close friend.

Do you (or maybe *did you*):

- End both relationships, saying you can never trust either of them ever again?

- Feel it's possible you have contributed to this double betrayal in some way or another?
- Wrack your brains for exactly where you went wrong?

Of course, there is no right or wrong answer to this question; it depends entirely on where you're coming from. You might well jump from one option to another, but deep down one of the choices will feel more familiar to you than the others...

Awareness has got to help enormously. Now you've answered the question, you may know which camp you fall into. Turn the question onto your own life. Is there anyone out there that you're blaming for the end of your relationship? Alternatively, in your own world, what are you blaming yourself for?

Task 11: Who Do You Blame?

In this 15-minute task, you need to record your thoughts and become aware of your blame game.

As a Relate-trained couples counsellor, I soon learned about marital fits. It's where people have got together because consciously and/or unconsciously they recognise each other, perhaps before they even know **15 min** whether or not they take sugar in their tea.

By recognition, I mean they are attracted because the person feels so familiar in some ways, probably because they have traits similar to those of the adults who brought them up. Opposites attract too, of course; wanting something they don't feel they have in themselves. So, blamers and blamees are going to be subconsciously attracted to each other, aren't they? Why wouldn't they be? It really suits a blamer to have someone up close and personal on whom he or she can blame everything that goes wrong.

Likewise, it fits with the blamee who is utterly used to blaming him- or herself for everything that's not right. 'Give me your s*** and I'll carry it for you!' says the blamee unconsciously. Very neat and tidy on the surface then, but what a horrendous mess underneath. A marriage made in hell.

The roots for both blamers and blamees (B&Bs from now on) will undoubtedly go back to their families of origin. And with a bit of detective work, it won't take long to locate the problem.

Until recently, I fell into the category of blamee. Most blamees have been traumatised as children. My default position was if something was wrong then it must be my fault. I can see where it all started, but I know it's not all my fault in my heart (as well as in my head) now.

Blamees typically suffer with low self-worth. Furthermore, they will always feel not good enough and will often feel downright bad. None of which are good ingredients in relationships with ourselves or indeed others.

On researching my B&B subject, I found people who take the blame for everything are often highly sensitive and – naturally enough – have a tendency to be over-responsible. You're not kidding – and it's an exhausting way to live! Heaping layer upon layer of blame upon themselves, blamees carry so much unnecessary heavy luggage around all the time.

Many Blamers, on the other hand, have also been traumatised as children but they choose the flip side of the coin to express it. They may really struggle with accepting certain things that have happened. It's just too scary for them to look at themselves, so it has to be someone else's fault. They can't admit their failings, and haven't learned to take responsibility for their actions. They are self-appointed 'victims' of other people's behaviour and they often feel helpless and out of control. Many go on to become control freaks as a direct result.

They are prone to 'splitting' too. They will choose to make someone 'all good' or 'all bad' in their heads instead of accepting that there's a bit of good in the worst of us, and a bit of bad in the best of us!

Both B&Bs may well have emotional neglect in their backgrounds but the way forward is to acknowledge this – as uncomfortable as it may be to face it – and make the decision that as an adult, you will now choose to treat yourself with love and care. *No more neglect.*

Blamers need to take back their projections and see the huge benefits of taking their fair share of responsibility as adults. The next time they find themselves blaming someone, they need to remember that they will get so much more out of calming right down and committing to looking at the situation with complete honesty. As an example: 'She's let me down again. Women always let me down! They are not to be trusted.' If a man finds himself saying this again and again, then he'd better start owning where those feelings originate from, or he'll keep repeating his pattern. Once he understands where he came from, and what he needs to change, he will be in a much better position to make healthy relationships. It will transform his life.

Blamees need to become realistic and offload inappropriate responsibility. 'I always pick the wrong men!' was one of my refrains until it just occurred to me that the men in question had a say in our relationships too! I used to blame myself entirely for my choices, but it does take two to tango. However, I was horribly drawn to emotionally unavailable men because it was what I grew up with, and so therefore it felt very familiar.

B&Bs have often both had difficulties in accepting their powerlessness as children, and have consequently gone into survival mode. At some level, a blamer can be subconsciously frightened of annihilation – as strong as that sounds – if he or she owns up to anything, and a blamee can be subconsciously frightened of annihilation if he or she gets anything wrong. They are also scared to face the horror that someone they loved so much caused them so much pain.

But we're grown-ups now and we need to shed outdated (and now unhelpful) coping mechanisms. We also need to STOP blaming, altogether, be it other people or ourselves. Let's look at responsibility instead, and make decisions with our adult heads to heal our child hearts.

The blame game

Task 12 for Blamers: Take Stock

15 min Look at your part in your divorce. Halt your automatic reaction to blame someone else and instead look at what led to what… Which bits are *you* responsible for? For example, if the marriage floundered because of constant rowing, then decide it takes two to argue, and that you both have a point of view? Look at how you could have done things differently, which might have resulted in a discussion rather than a row.

Task 13 for Blamees: Think Carefully

15 min When you're upset, halt your automatic reaction to take on all the responsibility for what's happened. Be realistic and work out who is responsible for what. Own your part but look at how others might have contributed in some way. For example, your ex is giving you the cold shoulder and has not replied to your loving request to ease the tensions between you and find a healthy way forward. The old you might immediately blame yourself. But if the new you's conscience is clear, then simply accept that he/she has his/her own reasons for behaving like that, which are all about them – and not about you.

The Rewards For Both B&Bs

When you become aware of your B&B tendencies, and take appropriate steps to work them through, the rewards will be endless. There will be growth, insight, and better relationships with others and yourself. You will become unstuck, and you will find yourself moving forward in all sorts of ways. You will undoubtedly have a much better and happier life, which will have a positive, knock-on effect on others too.

I do like a happy ending!

Herewith a quote:

> To be free people we must assume total
> responsibility for ourselves, but in doing so we must
> possess the capacity to reject responsibility that is
> not truly ours.
>
> **M. Scott Peck,**
> **Meditations from the Road**

Deborah took a long time to embrace forgiveness. "I was the loyal, doting wife of 25 years. My husband and I had a child, and I was a step-mother to two of his from a previous marriage. Then, he just announced he wanted a divorce. Very quickly he hooked up with an old friend of his, a recent widow."

Deborah reflects, "How dare this happen to me? How could I be *discarded* like this? The anger and resentment festered within me for years. Even when I moved on, and found a wonderful new partner – the way I had been treated still affected me deeply. It was as though some kind of judgement had been passed on me, and I had no real way to fight back."

Deborah continues: "What I needed, far earlier in the process, was to move on and stop his actions from affecting my thinking. I would bad-mouth my former husband to friends, and it impacted our relationships. If I had realised the power of forgiveness and letting go sooner, I would have avoided what were pointless and wasted years of internal anguish, anger and bitterness. The past is the past; let it go."

CHAPTER SIX: THE DESTRUCTIVE POWER OF GUILT

Guilt is so destructive if left to its own devices. It will play havoc with you, and your life, and have you riding round and round the same old ground until you break the cycle.

Beating yourself up over and over again for something you did (or didn't do), thought (or didn't think), will achieve nothing except severe emotional bruising.

We cannot change the past, no matter how much we want to. We cannot go back and right wrongs, no matter how much we'd love to. If we want to live good, useful lives then we've got to be as strong as we can be, not so wounded with self-flagellation that we're unable to be at our best.

'But I don't deserve to be happy!' you might think. Who says? You? I used to think I didn't deserve happiness, until I came to know better; now, I hope to guide you to banishing the destructive and pernicious power of inappropriate and neurotic guilt.

This 'not deserving' business is a horrible, evil weed that once planted, can grow like wildfire. That which we feed – flourishes. We must never forget that feelings are not facts!

Do you know the story about the grandfather telling his grandsons to feed the right wolf? The parable tells us how we have two wolves living inside each of us – a good one and a bad one – and they will inevitably get into a terrible fight. 'So who will win, grandfather?' ask the two boys. The old man smiles and simply says, 'The one you feed.'

I love this story and today I can grasp it emotionally, as well as intellectually.

Which one needs feeding?

I know a lot about guilt because I fed the wrong wolf for so very long. And many of you reading this will strongly identify with that. What the hell were we – are we – doing to ourselves?!? I can tell you now. By feeding that bad wolf, it grows bigger and bigger by the day. I did it repeatedly, to the extent that I turned it into a serious habit, if not an addiction. Feeding the bad wolf regularly creates a neural pathway that has guilt written all the way through it like a stick of rock.

Guilt is helpful if it teaches us something. If we know we've done something wrong, we can make our apologies and hopefully learn from it. And that is where we should leave it. I guess some people are able to do that, but there are many of us who don't. Do we think we're earning brownie points by suffering over and over and over again?

In families, we often carry generations of baggage, without even being aware of it, or what it is. I suspect guilt was part of my family tree among other unhelpful traits. As humans, we are all prone to loyalty to the tapestry of the past, sometimes for good and sometimes for bad.

When we look at our own guilty feelings, there's a lot we need to become aware of, especially when we have been prone to self-flagellation.

To illustrate what I'm on about, herewith a real case history – obviously, I've changed the names. The story is not about divorce, per se. But it is about something that many people going through divorce will recognise: the end of a relationship when one person walks out.

Peter, 49, is married with two grown-up children. When he was 18, his girlfriend Samantha, 21, became pregnant and decided she was going to have the baby with or without him. He felt far too young to cope with the responsibility, and told her exactly that, but said he would try to knuckle down. The couple moved in together and when their baby boy, Tom, was born, they were absolutely delighted. Peter gave up the idea of university because he needed to earn money fast. When their baby was a year old, Peter and Sam's relationship began to crack seriously.

'We'd only been together a few months when Sam got pregnant,' he explains. 'So we didn't exactly know each other very well. Living together was quite difficult and then, when Tom came along, the pressures seemed enormous. Looking back, I suppose I also felt resentful that I didn't go to Uni, and I felt envious of all my mates who apparently seemed to be enjoying life, being free and single. Sam veered between being very lovey-dovey with me and then tearful and hostile. I loved my son, but I don't quite know what I felt about Sam. Trapped, I suppose… which was very unfair of me.'

Basically, what has tormented Peter for years, is that he 'did a runner' shortly after Tom's second birthday. He moved to America from the UK and rejected all of Sam's efforts to reconnect.

'I feel absolutely terrible about it. I behaved abominably. Totally and utterly selfishly. Tom is 30 now and I haven't seen him since he was two-years-old. He's never tried to find me, to my knowledge – and why would he? I abandoned him and his mother and never contributed anything financially or otherwise to his growing up.'

Peter still lives in America, having fallen in love with Susie, a woman he met when he was 27. They married and had two daughters. With Susie's support, he tracked down his son and Tom's mother and tried to make amends.

'I saw the light when my daughters were little. I saw how much they benefitted from having two parents around and I was riddled with guilt about Tom. I missed him too, and longed to see him to try and make it up to him in some way or another.'

Sadly, all Peter's efforts were starkly rejected and while he understands that entirely, he cannot forgive himself for what he did.

Peter needs to forgive himself. The guilt is eating him up.

Peter made a mistake, a pretty big one, and of course he felt awful about it at the time. Those feelings got worse as he got older and wiser, and when he had his epiphany he went all out to try and right his wrong. He is genuinely sorry; deeply remorseful about his behaviour back then. Of course, it's healthy to feel those emotions, and anybody in his situation with a conscience would have similar feelings. But once you have been through the grief, the guilt, and remorse, and have made your amends, the healthy thing would be to let it go.

In Peter's case, there are a lot of other things that are coming in to play. He has hangover guilt from his family of origin. He was the youngest of four boys and felt his parents were disappointed with him from the start for not being a girl. His father was an alcoholic, who was always letting the family down and his mother was also emotionally unavailable in her own way. He grew up feeling guilty, thinking he was somehow to blame for all the chaos at home.

Simply speaking, had Peter come from a more stable background a) he may have been responsible about contraception and b) he would have been far better equipped to cope with an unplanned baby when he arrived.

Instead, he simply didn't know how to handle the consequences of his actions. He did what he thought was best at the time. He was running scared. He told himself that there was every chance Sam and Tom would be better off without him.

Unless Peter does something about his sack load of guilt, he is depriving himself, and his family, of a much happier version of himself. His true self – the man he is meant to be.

Yes, Peter violated his own moral code but today he is not the young man he was then. He wouldn't dream of behaving like that now.

If you feel you were the person responsible for the end of your marriage, when you walked out, then one vital step is to forgive yourself. You're aware of your actions and you're not in denial. Now though, you need to recognise that the past is the past, and it must not eat you up in the present.

Task 14: Spot the Difference!

Pick just one thing you are feeling guilty about (I know there might be many!). Draw up two columns, one called OBVIOUS GUILT, the other named HANGOVER GUILT and fill them in appropriately.

15 min For example, 'I feel guilty for all the times I disparaged and humiliated my partner in public.' The second column will relate to all the guilty feelings you've always had about your public behaviour at the time. Now, do the same for everything you feel guilty about currently.

Peter (mentioned above) is a different person today. We so often judge our past with who we are now. If we'd known then what we know

now, we might well have done things differently. We did what we did based on who we were *then*. Had we known better, we would have had more options, more choices.

Wikipedia offers a really spot-on definition of guilt: 'Guilt is a cognitive or an emotional experience that occurs when a person believes or realises – accurately or not – that he or she has compromised his or her own standards of conduct or has violated a universal moral standard and bears significant responsibility for that violation.'

I like the way it says 'accurately or not'. You might not feel guilty about something I have felt awful about, and vice versa. Our perceptions are just that – perceptions. I love the quote usually attributed to Anais Yin, and sometimes to Carl Jung. *We do not see things as they are – we see them as we are.*

We are all human and we all make mistakes. Very big ones sometimes. But we all need to remember that whatever it was, it does not define us. We are not our bad deed, word, or thought. We are multi-faceted. Remember, whatever we focus on, gets bigger. If we added up the amount of time we have spent on our guilt it would astound and horrify us. Imagine if we'd spent that time on something constructive – yes, enough to fuel a rocket or two. Let's look at it this way: imagine if we had put all that focus and energy on celebrating the loving, kind, compassionate and creative part of ourselves? Wow!

NB: Feed the good wolf!

Task 15: Acknowledge the Good

Make a list of all your qualities. Then think again and add to it because you're quite likely to have missed many out. *Now bask in them*!

Ask someone you really know and trust what your qualities are. Add them to your list if they're not already there.

15 min

Moving on, George explains here about his journey of forgiveness. "My ex-wife, let's call her Marcie, had two main problems. One, she had a need to appear healthy, wealthy, and successful *all the time*. Two, she would spend beyond our means to achieve it. Thanks to social media, the internet became awash with glamorous photos from restaurants, shops, and holiday locations.

"I was earning a good salary but her spending began to eat away at my sanity. It came to a point where I began to break down physically under the stress of worrying about our debts. Whenever I tried to get a serious handle on the family's finances, I would be undermined by more of her spending.

"For my mental health, I knew I needed out, but I was wracked with guilt because I felt like I'd deserted her. It feels like I walked out on her when, really, I had no other course of action. Self-forgiveness was the start of my path to recovery."

CHAPTER SEVEN: THE STIFLING POWER OF SHAME

Shame is an insidious feeling that many of us have experienced on many occasions. The triggers can be major or minor, and the shame feelings that come up and envelop us can be overwhelming.

We want to run, hide, dissolve – escape!

Unless addressed, shameful feelings can stay with us long after their sell-by date. We feel undressed!

The difference between shame and guilt needs to be clarified for this chapter.

Fossum and Mason say in their book *Facing Shame* that, 'While guilt is a painful feeling of regret and responsibility for one's actions, shame is a painful feeling about oneself as a person.'

Guilt is what we suffer when we feel awful about something we've done, whereas shame is the feeling we have about *who we are*. Shame is a hideous trap to be caught in, but you can find your way out.

NB: If you feel shameful, you're going to be very vulnerable to feeling neurotically guilty.

I do love an acronym because they quickly remind us what's important. I've come up with one for SHAME – Seek Help And Master Enemy!

It is shame that says we're not good enough. It is shame that leads us into self-abuse. Philosopher Jean-Paul Sartre described shame as a 'haemorrhage of the soul' and that is pretty much what it feels like.

When we're in shame, we feel awful. Hot with humiliation and a total disregard of self-worth. It is a very miserable place to be. It also keeps us disconnected from our Higher Power. Guilt (in a way) feels better, because there's a sense – sometimes – that maybe we can make amends; but when we're in shame, we feel there's nowhere to go.

Once more, it's time for the Feel, Deal, and Heal strategy. And the first tool you need is compassion.

I realised only a few years ago that I grew up feeling 'faulty'. A characteristic that carried through my life.

And again, I now know I'm in very good company. Many of us grew up feeling exactly the same, with a shocking lack of self-worth. If your upbringing was a bit chaotic, to say the least, feelings of shame will have been reinforced at regular intervals.

Even if you had a pretty idyllic childhood, you would have very likely felt shame at some point. If you were the last to be picked for the netball or football team, or not picked at all, you might have felt the hand of shame tapping on your shoulder.

People who are familiar with shame can be so self-critical and readily blame themselves. So if you're someone who finds it incredibly hard to forgive yourself, look closely at the subject of shame because it is figuring heavily for you. And no doubt you have neglected yourself and indeed abandoned yourself at many points in your life.

Men and women who were abused as children will nearly always have experienced a huge sense of shame as a result. The tragedy, of course, is that a part of them feels the abuse was their fault. And, of course, it wasn't their fault AT ALL. While some may know that intellectually, many victims of abuse struggle to know that truth in their heart. This can stop them from reaching their full potential as adults and can also lead to a continuing cycle of abuse, either as victims or perpetrators. Other forms of abuse – mental, physical and emotional – will also produce shame.

Shame is responsible for so many problems and it can lead to all kinds of self-destructive behaviours and thinking. So let's start tackling it!

Task 16 Expose your Shame

15 min

Remember my acronym for SHAME - Seek Help And Master Enemy! Bring it out from the dark and into the light. Internalised shame needs to be flushed out and healed, and once you become aware of it, you will see it has been very destructive for you. Look at your sense of shame with the help of a therapist or wise friend and see where it originates. Abandonment or abuse issues might be relevant here.

Feelings such as being unlovable, or useless, or undeserving will be shame-based and do not belong to you. They have no place in your life. You ARE lovable, you are certainly far from useless, and you DESERVE to be free from the layers of shame that simply do not belong to you.

If you have been prone to shame, then beware of narcissists (okay, this may be a bit late, now). These poor creatures cannot bear to look at their shame issues and will often project them onto their partner (i.e., 'make' you feel the shame for them).

Mabel, 45, was married for 15 years to Rob and she felt riddled with shame whenever she had too much to drink. 'He hated me drinking and would get very unpleasant about it. I gave up drinking, thinking it would be a good thing to do for the marriage, but he didn't give up his gambling habit. When he could no longer shame me for drinking, he started to pick on other things about me he wanted to change. I then started to suggest we think about parting because I couldn't save the marriage single-handedly. He simply said 'We can't afford to part'.'

Mabel made a few more attempts to part in an amicable way, but because of her own abandonment issues from childhood, she couldn't see it through.

'I think he saw the writing on the wall though, because as soon as he found someone else to go to, he left overnight without a backward glance which was pretty traumatic for me. He told me once he couldn't bear to be on his own and being the narcissist he is, he had no thought whatsoever for my feelings. He never did really – it was all about him.

'I've learned so much since we separated and divorced. It was painful at the time because it turned my world upside down and inside out – again. But it was the making of me really. I feel sorry for my ex, I really do. I chose to work on my childhood issues, but he chose not to. Neither of us had it easy as children. I really hope he's happy now, but unless he's found the courage to deal with his inherent shame issues, I don't see that he can be.'

It takes courage to look at shame and begin the process of forgiveness. Brene Brown says, 'If we share our story with someone who responds with empathy and understanding, shame can't survive.' But first, to Seek Help And Master Enemy, we have to find the willingness to tackle it.

Here, Alice talks about her shame. "My former husband and I had been together for a long time. The relationship had changed over the years, and was beginning to feel like it was going nowhere. We thought that getting married would solve the problem. We were wrong, and we ended up divorcing less than two years after saying our vows. My big fear, for a long time afterwards, was that our decision-making made us look stupid to friends and family. I thought that people would judge us, and retreated into my shell in embarrassment following the divorce.

"Ultimately, the only way that I was able to park that chapter of my life was by forgiving myself. Okay, my husband and I made the decision to get married and, okay, it didn't work out – but no-one got hurt. If people want to judge me (although I've mainly found that people don't concern themselves so much with my matters!) then let them. What I cannot do, is let my perceptions of other people – seeing me as foolish – inhibit me or hold me back. So I made a commitment to forgive my actions, and live with the consequences as a normal and full member of society!"

CHAPTER EIGHT: EMBRACE WILLINGNESS AND ENTHUSIASM

I always want to jump for joy when I see willingness and enthusiasm in anyone, including myself.

I know how powerful the qualities of willingness and enthusiasm are, and I have the utmost respect for anyone who is prepared to work with them. They are profoundly important assets, and they are available to anyone who chooses to use them. They also work in absolute harmony with the 15-Minute Rule.

In working on your 15-Minute Rule for Forgiveness, willingness and enthusiasm are two of the most helpful companions to take along for the journey. And if you can't conjure them up naturally, I can help you to locate them.

Just to make it absolutely clear, willingness is about wanting to do something or, if you can't manage that, then wanting to want to!

> It is our attitude at the beginning of a difficult task which, more than anything else, will affect its successful outcome.
>
> **William James, Psychologist**

Now you might be loaded with willingness and enthusiasm for tackling your forgiveness issues – 'bring it on!' you might be shouting, ready to embrace it wholeheartedly – but, on the other hand, you may be a bit lacking in this department. In which case, I can encourage you to plant the seeds and grow them.

By the way, the word enthusiasm comes from the Greek *Enthusiasmos* which means to be inspired or possessed by a divine being. We all know enthusiasm when we see it, and indeed experience it. Healthy enthusiasm is very contagious, constructive, and charismatic.

Willingness and enthusiasm create momentum and the first letters of each word spell WE. We can do this – and we can do it together! To my absolute delight, there is now an award certificate, for Willingness and Enthusiasm, handed out to cadets in a disadvantaged youth program in Melbourne, Australia. They very kindly dedicated it to me, after my TEDx talk inspired them. Let's hope I can inspire you to grab hold of the WE word.

Resistance Removal

If you have any resistance to finding willingness and enthusiasm to tackle the problem of forgiveness then the first thing to do is ask yourself why. *Please* don't shy away from the question; instead, find the courage to look deep inside.

If answers come quickly, then you've made fabulous progress. If you're digging your heels in, and refusing to move on this, let me offer some suggestions.

Does it feel like it's too much work? Okay, take it gently, 15 minutes at a time.

Are you frightened that it's going to be too painful? It won't be nearly as painful as carrying your baggage around for the rest of your life.

Are you fearful of change and only now beginning to admit that? Let me tell you a story... I used to fantasise about packing up all my troubles, especially those around self-forgiveness, and letting them go up, up and away on helium balloons. But then, very soon after that delicious thought, I experienced huge fear. With the benefit of hindsight, I realised it seemed safer to hang on to the troubles than let go of them. Of course it did, because that was my familiar position! It was horrible but I knew it, I recognised it, and it had been part of me for a very long time. Change was SCARY, even though – intellectually – I knew it would be beneficial. However, I was lagging far behind emotionally.

Now, years later, having done my forgiveness work, my emotions have caught up. I am now pleased to report that when I fantasise about my troubles going up, up and away on those helium balloons, I feel fabulous! As light as air, and free. Free!

Let it all go

So how can you find the willingness to forgive yourself, or another person, when there appears to be little or none? You need to listen to that voice within, be it your Higher Power, or your wise parent self. It is the child in you who might be struggling to forgive. While you need to listen to that child with love and respect, she or he needs to know that there is a safe grown-up in charge.

Case Study: Mandy

Mandy suffered a hideous double betrayal when her husband went off with her sister. 'It was a complete nightmare that blew my family apart,' she says. 'Luckily there were no children involved. My sister and I had got married within months of each other, but just a couple of years down the line, my husband suggested we swap partners for a while. He said he could live with my sister and her husband could move in with me! We could then swap back at some point.

'As you can imagine I was absolutely horrified. My sister swore she knew nothing about it but I felt I couldn't trust anyone after that. I moved back in with my mum but, of course, she was caught in the middle of her two daughters. She believed my sister wasn't aware of my husband's suggestion but I wasn't so sure. I was right – shortly after I left my husband, he moved in with my sister.'

The next two years were very difficult for Mandy. She and her sister's husband commiserated with each other but when he suggested they become a couple to 'keep things neat and tidy' she felt beside herself with anger.

'But then we saw the funny side and ended up having a laugh,' says Mandy. 'It actually felt quite good to find the humour in an awful situation.'

From that day on, Mandy felt it was time to start turning a corner. 'I was sick of being miserable and sick of seeing my mum so unhappy with the situation. I'd met Caroline through a friend and decided to work her 15-Minute Rule for Forgiveness.'

The rest, as they say, is history! Mandy had planted the seed of willingness and enthusiasm, because she desperately wanted to feel better.

'Once I had made the decision to work Caroline's book I was already in a much better place,' she says. 'That then revved up my enthusiasm to carry on and I'm so glad I did.

'I am very pleased to say I forgave my sister, although that didn't mean I wanted a relationship with her. However, when my ex dumped her and ran off with someone else, I had to forgive myself for thinking it served her right!

'Double betrayals are so awful. Two people you love have done the dirty on you. And the thought of them snuggling up together is hell. All that is behind me now. I forgave them both and I am free from carrying that pain around with me. I have compassion for them both today – my sister and my ex have a lot to learn and I don't see how either of them will find happiness until they are willing to do so. Neither one of them has apologised to me for their actions. I don't need that now but it would be nice!'

Letting go of pain is not easy, but boy is it necessary for peace of mind. A friend once told me to think of letting go as posting a letter. If you want it to go then you cannot hang on to a corner of the envelope. You'll be stuck there until you do.

What does the word willingness suggest to you? To me, it means someone who is cheerfully up for new ideas and who is happy to help themselves or others on the road to a happier life. We all know God loves a trier! We humans love a trier too.

Now, what does the word unwilling mean to you? To me, it conjures up a grumpy, surly, moody person, with a reluctance or aversion to helping anyone out, including him- or herself.

So who would you rather be? And who would you rather be with?

But how do you cultivate willingness? You start by imagining all the benefits that will soon be coming your way if you commit to your chosen task. Again, use the 15-Minute Rule and update your list about why you want to invite forgiveness into your life. It only takes one nudge to get that ball rolling and then it gathers momentum, with enthusiasm kicking in along the way. It's such exciting energy!

> Nobody gets to the top of the mountain without falling on his face over and over again.
>
> **Jen Sincero**

Task 17: Trust

15 min

Using the 15-Minute Rule, look at your list of fears and challenge some of your outdated beliefs that have been holding you back from fabulous forgiveness. Then start thinking about trusting your Higher Power, the Universe, or Love.

Please be willing to trust that there is something out there greater than us. If for some reason you are unwilling to do that, then have enough respect for yourself to ask why. If you are still unwilling, having had a good conversation with yourself, then I suggest you 'fake it to make it' and set yourself a 21-day exercise to suspend your judgements on this matter. Then choose to believe there is something out there greater than you. Take the risk – I dare you! Dare to change your habitual way of thinking.

If, on the other hand, you're already in touch with a power greater than yourself, then become really willing to trust it.

When your fear pops up, see it for what it is. You may be so used to feeling fearful that it has become your 'normal'. Again, so much of it is habitual; it's time you started really looking at it.

We can say farewell to our old and redundant fears now. We are adults, believe it or not, and those old childish fears that helped us survive are now in the past.

Now for Enthusiasm...

Enthusiasm is a wonderful quality and, as I said earlier, it's very contagious. It bounces off people and can be very attractive. We can both give it off and be drawn to it, and it's a joyful place to be. Charismatic people are usually enthusiastic people. The heady combination of willingness and enthusiasm is what makes all the difference between achieving what we desire and giving up before we even get started. These two things propel us towards our goals and encourage us beautifully. The WE concept (Willingness and Enthusiasm) is a real joy to work with.

If your enthusiasm for finding forgiveness is a bit sluggish, then rev it up by again visualising just how happy and free you will be when you let go of all the pain you have been lugging around with you.

Then take action and make the decision to go forward on the constructive path. Become willing to do so regardless of the 'Yes, buts' and 'What ifs?'. Use your Adult self to reassure your Child self.

The real
secret
to success is
enthusiasm

When you're in full enthusiasm mode, you'll know what a great place it is to be.

If it starts to slow down sometimes, there is no need to worry. Think of it as an exercise bike that tells you to pedal faster if you're slowing down or you will lose the programme. The 15-Minute Rule is much kinder than that. Once you've started your Forgiveness work, you can either keep pedalling or pause and pick up later where you left off.

Now imagine yourself tackling a task with lots of willingness and enthusiasm and then imagine yourself tackling the same task without them. Think how much you'd be missing out by not embracing these two fabulous powerhouses! You have so much to gain by grabbing them with both hands.

Task 18: Time To Get Motivated!

To rev you up further, let's celebrate your willingness and enthusiasm today. Write down three projects you would like to become enthusiastic about and willing to tackle.

15 min On a scale of 1 to 10, with 10 being excellent (and 1 being not so hot), rate the willingness and enthusiasm you currently feel about each project. Look at your score, think about your attitude to each one, and try reframing things. For example, instead of saying 'I haven't got the energy for it' try saying 'Energy breeds energy'. In other words, check the way you're thinking about it. If it's negative, then change it to positive.

Now think about those projects again and see if your ratings have changed.

Just to let you know, I soon discovered that even boring chores become almost a pleasure within the safe timeframe of my 15-Minute Rule!

Case Study: Lizzie

Lizzie, 38, had been unwilling to even think about forgiving her ex-fiancé, Ryan, for jilting her seven weeks before their wedding. When he told her he simply couldn't go through with it because he feared being 'trapped', she was devastated.

'I did everything I could to reassure him that it wasn't a trap, that we loved each other and we were free to make the choice to be together,' says Lizzie. 'That's when he said he was choosing not to get married but he'd be happy for us to continue living together.

'I couldn't do that and so he moved out and left me to cancel all the wedding plans which was so painful.'

Months of turmoil followed and then there were talks of reconciliation.

'He begged to come back,' says Lizzie, 'but my pride wouldn't let me forgive him. A friend of mine advised me to at least have some willingness to think about forgiveness.

'Once I made the decision to do that, enthusiasm began to creep in. All sorts of possibilities suddenly came into view which then made me more willing and more enthusiastic!'

Lizzie's friend then suggested to her that she shouldn't take Ryan's decision not to get married personally.

'In the old days I would have screamed at her for that statement, but by then I was open enough in my heart to take that on board. I really began to see it wasn't personal, that Ryan's reluctance to make that marriage commitment stemmed from his childhood and his parents' ugly divorce.'

Lizzie has forgiven Ryan now and he has recently moved back in.

There is no talk of weddings but they have committed to couple counselling.

Ryan is now struggling to forgive himself for the pain he put Lizzie through. He has come to understand that the need to forgive himself started long before he hurt Lizzie.

Another essential component in the wonderful world of willingness and enthusiasm is compassion. Please, please, throw away the stick that you beat yourself up with on a regular basis. It is useless; in fact, it's a darn sight worse than useless – it seriously damages your health. If you can't be bothered to work on your forgiveness project, or if you're down in the dumps or depressed, or if you haven't done what you intended to, do you really think you need the stick? Of course not. What you need is an emotional boost, one that you can give yourself. Talk to yourself nicely, soothingly; tell yourself 'all will be well' and 'you are able to do this'. Pray if you have faith; meditate; nurture and care for yourself, and feel confident that you will find the motivation – the willingness and enthusiasm – to do what you need to do.

A willingness to make changes for the better is huge growth. Pure and simple.

CHAPTER NINE: THE POWER OF SAYING SORRY

'Love means never having to say you're sorry' is a catchphrase from the Erich Segal novel *Love Story*, made even more famous by the film starring Ryan O'Neal and Ali MacGraw. Was that line so popular because it was a quick fix to do away with guilt? Quick fixes don't work for long, of course...

On the other hand, a genuine apology is love in action. And it spreads.

It's like throwing a golden pebble into the water and watching the ripples go far and wide, way beyond what our eyes can see.

Saying sorry, and meaning it, is incredibly powerful. Hearing sorry, and knowing it's meant, means the world.

Simon and Garfunkel would benefit hugely, as would their many fans, if they could say sorry to each other. Art Garfunkel has been quoted saying, 'I never forget, and I never forgive.' They have their grievances about each other and they're not prepared to let them go. How sad is that?

Task 19: Who Needs An Apology?

15 min Make a list of who you think deserves an apology from you. (Apart from a former partner, it might include friends or work colleagues you dumped on, or maybe an 'in-law', or maybe the workman who caught you on a bad day.) Please make sure your own name is there! If you have one, you might want to put your Higher Power, on there too.

Once you've done your list, ask a tried and trusted friend to talk it through with you. You may have forgotten some people, or there may be names on there that aren't appropriate. You don't need to apologise if you haven't done anything wrong.

There may be others who need to go on there – whom you haven't put down – because you both did wrong to each other. Here's where we need to apologise for the wrong we did, despite what they did to us.

Or what we perceived they did. As they say in 12-step programmes, we need to keep *our side of the street clean.* They also say that if an apology is likely to do more harm than good, then we leave it out.

Generally speaking, saying sorry – and meaning it – will not only be music to the ears of the person who's hearing it, but you will also just love the harmonious feelings it brings *to you.*

Just imagine how you would feel if you received a genuine apology from someone who has done you wrong. It would soothe you, calm you, put out the fire or melt the ice that surrounds the person and the problem in your head.

If you hadn't forgiven them, you might choose to do so right now. Or at least plant the seeds for the forgiveness fruit to flourish.

Every time we offer a heartfelt apology, we are contributing to the peace of mind of another, the world, and ourselves. Good begets good. Love begets love. Forgiveness begets forgiveness.

The person on the receiving end of your apology will begin to feel empathy for you and their hurt will start to heal. The natural order of things means they will start to entertain thoughts of forgiveness.

To inspire you, take note of the following quote by Donald L. Hicks.

'When you forgive, you free your soul. But when you say I'm sorry, you free two souls.'

And here's one by Sanjo Jendayi:

'Sometimes, an apology sets free a part of you that you didn't even realise was caged… and forgiveness destroys the cage.'

If you're carrying guilt around about someone who is no longer with us, you can still make your amends. Send up a prayer for it to be passed on, or write a letter. Part of the grief process is worrying about things that were said, or indeed left unsaid. You can be sure the departed have forgiven us and it makes nothing but sense for us to forgive ourselves.

Now if you're anything like me, you've got a lot of apologising to do to yourself and your HP! Say sorry for how hard you've been on yourself, the person you have beaten up over and over again. Say sorry to your HP for how you've abused yourself.

We can make our amends by deciding to treat ourselves with love, forgiveness, compassion, care, and respect FROM THIS MOMENT ON!

Task 20: Let It Take Root

Take a timed 15 minutes for this to sink in. Write down anything you think will help you to start immediately loving, forgiving, and caring for yourself. (And stop trying to get it perfect!)

15 min

As Iyanla Vanzant says in her fabulous book *Until Today* 'Learn to love and honour yourself from the inside to the outside. More than this, our Creator has not asked of us.'

So how do you go about being good to yourself? You nurture and parent yourself, you become your own best friend, and you choose to turn negative thoughts and feelings into positive ones. Keep practising positive behaviours until they become habitual. You can start this by swapping your negative self-talk. For example, 'I just can't face all I have to do today – it's too much' could easily be swapped for 'I'm going to do what I can today and be nice to myself in the process!'

We've practised negative behaviours for so long that they feel normal. They're not.

Now, what about those of us who have continually and habitually said sorry when often we haven't done anything wrong whatsoever? Well that's got to stop!

It's only relatively recently that I've realised I'm not solely responsible for some of the difficulties in my life.

My ex-husband used to say: 'You're forever trying to make things right!' I looked at him in astonishment and my response was: 'Well somebody has to!'

Mmm, now I know it doesn't always have to be me. Looking back I was riddled with fear – as in, if I didn't do everything I could to make it all right, then the sky would fall in. This all goes back to feeling very unsafe as a child. Unless I could do everything in my power to make things ok, I feared disaster would happen.

Conversely, there are people who are incapable of saying sorry for anything. I have come to the conclusion that to do so is too frightening for them and on looking up this very subject, many therapists agree with me! These non-apologists are riddled with fear. For them, an apology means to expose their vulnerability, and their ego tells them it's too dangerous.

Matt, 47, told me about his complete inability to apologise until fairly recently. 'I couldn't bear to look back because my early life was far from easy. I wanted to forget the past and concentrate on looking forwards. I tried therapy once but I couldn't hack all that soul-searching. It was too painful. But then my relationship began to break down because of my drinking and I decided to quit and go to Alcoholics Anonymous meetings.

'I worked the Steps with my sponsor and when it became time to do Step Eight 'Make a list of all people we had harmed and became willing to make amends to them' I was ready for it.

'When I'd completed my Step Nine 'Made direct amends to such people wherever possible, except when to do so would injure them or others' I felt as if I'd shed a ton of weight. It was amazing – and still is!'

In further discussion, Matt revealed he had found the courage to look at his past and it wasn't nearly as frightening as he had imagined. 'It was much more manageable than I ever thought it would be,' he said. 'I've learned so much from it and it's enabled me to make some very positive changes.'

I've always loved that Katherine Mansfield quote: *'Fear is in the waiting room.'* Matt says he totally agrees with it!

Sometimes, we have to look back to go forward in the best way we can. Think of it as a driving analogy. When you're in your car, of course you're looking forward, but you're keeping an eye on your rear view mirror to avoid dangerous decisions and trouble hitting you from behind.

When two people decide to get a divorce, it isn't a sign that they 'don't understand' one another, but a sign that they have, at least, begun to.

Helen Rowland

CHAPTER TEN: OUT WITH THE OLD AND IN WITH THE NEW

We need to break old and outdated patterns and build lovely new ones. And there will be many around forgiveness.

So where did your recent issues with forgiveness begin? When your husband ran off with your best friend? When your wife disappeared virtually overnight, taking the children? When your ex left you penniless? When you violated your own moral code? All really difficult things to deal with but, as I've suggested earlier, for a lot of people, the roots to your *lack of forgiveness* were probably planted a long time before these very painful events.

Here's where we need to look, again, at your childhood wounds and find out where some of your forgiveness issues began. Many of them will stem from simply (but painfully) not feeling good enough. Many feelings of guilt took root here, and you need to have faith that you can dig them up and discard them.

I suggest that, even if you do not think that forgiveness issues originated from an earlier time in life, that you give this chapter a go. If you ultimately conclude that your childhood is not a root cause of current forgiveness issues – that is fine. But going through the process, here, is important.

Task 21: So Where Did It All Begin?

Spend time listing where your wounds originated. For example, was it the day your parents split up? The many times your dad didn't turn up to visit? The countless times you were let down by one or other of them? The abuse – physical, mental or sexual – you suffered at their hands or from someone else within the family or outside of it? The neglect? Since you picked up this book, you may already have a clearer picture of those early wounds. As painful as some of them are, knowledge is power and it's good to get it down in writing.

15 min

For me, separation anxiety started at two-years-old when my father disappeared. It was then compounded by spells in hospital for eye operations in the days when parents could only visit for an hour a day. I had the first op around the time my father left home. More separation, more pain. I soon sussed that visiting time was over the second I saw the table in my children's ward being laid for tea. 'Tablecloth, tablecloth!' I would shriek, bursting into tears. I knew it meant I was about to be ripped away from my mum. Again.

The word 'tablecloth' became part of the family vocabulary – meaning painful separation. 'It's tablecloth time,' my mother would say, often, when we were saying our goodbyes.

It might have been at that time, or when I was seven, that I tried to escape from hospital. I literally got to a door onto the street when a nurse grabbed me. Remembering this, as I do vividly, I look back and see just how distressed I must have been

Separation anxiety stayed with me until recently, and I had to truly acknowledge the original pain before I was able to let it go.

Remember this: if nothing changes, nothing changes. Or, to put it another way, if you keep on doing what you keep on doing, you will keep on getting what you keep on getting. It's as simple as that.

If you want something much better, then you're going to have to change something. Change! A scary word for many! But I promise you that once you see the benefits of change, it becomes much easier. You will begin to welcome change, to embrace it. You will be making new neural pathways in your brain that can only add to your happiness and well-being.

You have an ACE card, you know… this is an acronym I invented for Attitude Changes Everything.

Attitude Changes Everything

Your ACE card is a reminder that you can change your mindset, whenever you want, by adjusting how you want to think about something. You can bring out your ACE card any time you choose and with the right attitude, and The 15-Minute Rule, there will be no stopping you from making huge progress and achieving your dreams. Peace of mind being one of them.

It would obviously be enormously helpful for you to break destructive patterns in both thinking and behaviour. It's all perfectly possible, believe me.

Task 22: Now For The Solutions

15 min

Spend just 15 minutes brainstorming ways to create solutions to your problems. You can now start charting your positive future. Then go back to your solutions whenever you're ready and add to them. As I say to my daughter, and indeed to myself, 'Choose your thoughts wisely'. I came up with that phrase years ago, and I now use it as my screensaver! It reminds me – on a regular basis – that what we choose *to think* we are actually choosing *to feel.*

'Do you want to be right or do you want to be happy?' is a question we all need to ask ourselves from time to time. Of course, most of us often want to be both, but that's certainly not always possible. When you're dealing with a control freak, you're fighting a losing battle if you're trying to convince them you're in the right. You may well be right, but their control freakery just won't hear it. It's just too scary for them. They are so frightened of feeling 'less than others' so they go to the other extreme and tell themselves they are 'better than others'. So, I suggest you don't keep wasting your breath! What matters is you and your HP know the truth.

Arrogant or pompous folk are *always* right in their own minds and, of course, they can be a nightmare. We need to try to find compassion for them, because their arrogance or pomposity is simply a cover for their feelings of inferiority.

It reminds me of that old gag, 'When I married my Mr (or Mrs) Right, I didn't know his (her) first name was Always!'

Remember – a lot of our old thinking is so habitual. So, again, I say choose your thoughts wisely because you might be choosing old rubbish ones that really do not serve you well.

The Power of Habit

The power of habit makes me chuckle. Frequently. It took me ages to stop automatically looking for the time on my kitchen clock – even though I had removed it from that particular wall years ago!

As you read this next sentence, I urge you to pause for a second and ask yourself *what else* you're doing right now. Have you got a coffee in your hand? A glass of wine? A cigarette, a vape machine even? Is this question getting in the way of your next mouthful of scrummy pain au chocolat? In short, how much of what you are doing right now is habit?

The power of habit, as we know, is extraordinary – as many of our bad habits, or indeed old bad habits, testify. The fab news is that it's equally powerful for the good habits we've made and the ones we might be intending to pursue. So much of what we do is habitual, both consciously and unconsciously. I think we could really amuse – and shock ourselves – if we decide to become more aware of them… Ooh, I've just come up with a slogan: Be Aware or Beware!

Of course, there are all sorts of reasons why things can become a habit but let's focus on neural pathways for a moment. In essence, our brain makes stronger and stronger connections by repeatedly doing something until it becomes the new automatic.

Why do we do develop habits? And how can we change them? We can always change, even if you're like my ex-husband who doesn't believe in it.

Charles Duhigg is an award-winning New York Times reporter who wrote *The Power of Habit*. He says that, in the last decade, we've learned a lot about how habits work.

Apparently, there are three components to habit. It goes like this:

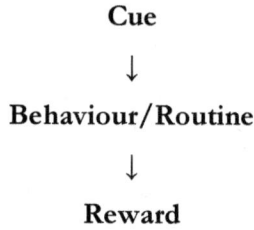

Cue

↓

Behaviour/Routine

↓

Reward

For example:

Cue [you feel stressed]

↓

Behaviour/Routine [you light a cigarette]

↓

Reward [you feel better]

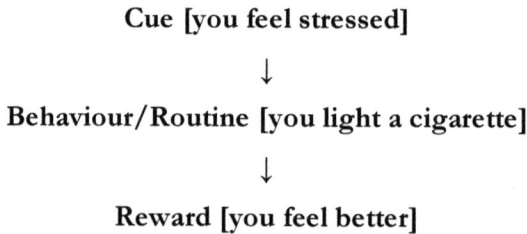

Your brain has associated the Cue and the Reward – and bingo, before long you have an addiction! In the past, people have concentrated on the Behaviour to change bad habits and while that is vitally important, we also need to pay huge attention to our Cues and Rewards. That is how habits occur and how we can change them.

'Over time, the Cue and Reward become more and more intertwined,' wrote Charles. 'That part of our brain, the basal ganglia, relates them together and the Behaviour/Routine that's associated with that almost happens automatically.'

The very good news is that we work well with Rewards. It has actually been proven that people are more likely to exercise regularly if they reward themselves with a small piece of chocolate afterwards. It might sound weird if we're exercising to lose weight, but apparently it works.

Who doesn't like a reward, especially when we feel we've worked hard and deserve one? As we know, virtue is its own reward, but it's a deserved bonus to give ourselves an extra one. And, of course, it's an excellent way to encourage our motivation to keep up the good work.

We're not daft; as we've already established, we enjoy things that make us feel good. That little piece of chocolate as mentioned above is a pleasurable reward for doing something healthy. The person has physically exercised, which will help lift their mood and then patted themselves on the back with a SMALL piece of chocolate. He/she has learned that a LITTLE bit of what you fancy does you good. However, if you can't stop at one SMALL piece of chocolate, then choose something else to reward yourself with!

Isabel, 37, has changed many habits using my 15-Minute Rule and the Reward concept has worked very well for her. She is now working the 15-Minute Rule for Forgiveness.

'I gave up smoking and a dreadful boyfriend with the 15-Minute Rule and a willingness to believe in something greater than myself!' she says.

'It was a great combination. Some days were much easier than others, that's for sure, but on those really difficult days I looked forward to my Reward and it helped keep me on track. I rode the waves of craving for nicotine, and craving for my ex, knowing that at 6pm I was giving myself the reward of an hour to do precisely what I wanted as long as it was healthy. Often it was watching a television programme I had recorded while painting my nails. Or it was getting under my duvet with whatever novel I was reading at the time. Occasionally, it was window-shopping online. I would turn off my phone and give it my full concentration. It was so relaxing for my brain!'

Isabel is very aware that changing a habit takes commitment. 'It's not plain sailing, but it is so worth it. I am now determined to forgive my ex for basically robbing me of my savings because, if I don't, I'm going to be screaming about the sheer injustice of his behaviour for years.

'I don't want to be obsessing about getting the money back from him, or endlessly wondering why he hasn't offered me a grovelling apology. He'll either make amends one day or he won't. I certainly don't want to be habitually worrying about it. I found the courage to leave him and now I need to forgive him, for my sake; otherwise, I'm still carrying him around with me!'

CHAPTER ELEVEN: LET GO OF YOUR WILLPOWER

You may think you could conquer this forgiveness thing if you could summon up enough willpower.

I used to think that.

We can all look back and recall when this so-called willpower worked or not. Dieting is something many of us are familiar with – and just how many times have you lost – and then regained – those same stones and pounds? Sometimes our so-called willpower worked successfully for a bit, but often it failed miserably. As for consistent, sustained willpower, well I don't see much of that around because we're flawed human beings.

There. I bet I've made your day now. You can relax! You can stop fretting about all the times your willpower deserted you and know that you are utterly and deliciously normal.

We have free will, yes, although some of us may find that hard to believe. I mean who is that gremlin that seems to take over and drive us to do things that masquerade as being against our will? Did I really polish off that tub of ice-cream the very night before my Weightwatchers weigh-in?

Many people find it baffling that they can be extremely determined in some areas of their life and very wobbly (literally!) in others. And they interpret this passivity as a failure to summon up willpower. But willpower is not something that can be summoned up; it is an illusion. Really!

So, what is the difference between thinking, 'I know I ought to, but it's just so hard' and 'I'm going to do this and nothing's going to stop me'? The secret is that …

DETERMINATION COMES FROM A SETTLED DECISION.

Now, of course, we are able to make some settled decisions with no problems whatsoever. These are the easy ones such as: 'Do I forgive that two-year-old for stamping on my foot?' 'Can I let go of that resentment about my friend being late for our outing?'

If we don't have mixed feelings about something, then the correct course of action is much more obvious. 'Would I allow George Clooney to kiss me?' Mmm, now that's a tough one… I'd love him to kiss me, repeatedly, but only if he weren't married and a dad to boot that is.

Ambivalence, then, is what we need to tackle head-on. Sorry, George!

'I know I ought to' screams of ambivalence. It immediately highlights the dilemma of knowing that we should do something while feeling reluctant to do so. What's more, we will probably revisit the dilemma frequently, each time telling ourselves 'I know I ought to,' or 'I know I ought NOT to' but still getting nowhere. We could probably fuel yet another rocket with all the energy we waste.

And, as I've said before, if we keep on doing what we keep on doing, we'll keep on getting what we keep on getting. So I guess it's time to do something differently…

Talk to reformed smokers and many of them, including me, will say they tried to give up many times before they succeeded. Some even bought into the myth that they just couldn't summon up the willpower to sustain it all those previous times but then, one day, bingo, they had success.

'All my unsuccessful attempts at giving up were part of my journey towards being a non-smoker,' said a close friend. Well, yes, that is absolutely true, but making a settled decision is likely to make our journey far shorter and less troublesome.

What's hugely important here (and again I repeat) is that *we don't have to wait for the feeling to make a decision!* I have discovered first-hand that if we put the action in first, then the feeling catches up.

I gave up smoking even though I didn't really want to. However, I wanted 'to want to' and that really helped. I made a decision and then I was happy to do it.

Now, let's apply this stuff to our excess baggage. For example, we might feel we need to get fitter, post-divorce. Again. We know we're going to be healthier, and slimmer, as a result and our confidence and self-esteem will benefit too. We can see all the plusses and are hard pushed to find any minuses.

But then our self-sabotage creeps in. 'I've tried to get fit many times – it doesn't work' or 'I'll start next Monday' or 'It's not fair – I have such a slow metabolism.'

Some people join a club, such as a running club, and find that groups are very helpful. When we enrol, we have actually made a settled decision. We are halfway to our goal when we walk through that door on our first visit.

So far so good. But let's say we have a wobble halfway through. How can we sustain our settled decision? We do this by reminding ourselves of all the benefits of positive change. We can look back and congratulate ourselves on how far we've come. We can reward ourselves with a timely treat. We can become aware of our self-sabotaging side…

If we don't do that, then we attempt to whip ourselves into shape by giving ourselves a really hard time for screwing up the program. What does this achieve? Another load of unhelpful shame! Self-forgiveness is essential for self-improvement, believe me.

According to Joseph Bikart, author of *The Art of Decision Making*, we each make 35,000 decisions a day on average. Think how much better life would be if the majority of them were good ones!

\   Good and evil both increase at compound interest.   /
That is why the little decisions you and I make every
day are of such infinite importance. The smallest
good act today is the capture of a strategic point
from which, a few months later, you may be able to
go on to victories you never dreamed of.

C.S. Lewis

But, far more seriously, in terms of forgiveness, how many zillions of times have you thought you *might* be better off forgiving someone – or forgiving yourself? So why not commit to doing so? *Today*, not one day in the distant future. Make the decision to embrace the idea of forgiveness today. It will be one of the best things you've ever done.

Task 23: How Long Has This Been Going On?

Look back to get an idea of how long you have struggled with the forgiveness issue. Write down any helpful associated thoughts and ideas. Can you remember when it all started? If you've discussed it with people, what help have they suggested? When you've been in touch with the idea of forgiveness, and the peace it can bring, how did you feel? What did your inner saboteur say to snatch it away again?

15 min

Now start using your parent/adult self to speak to your frightened inner child.

When the child in you says you'll have to see that person again if you forgive them, then put your arms around yourself and firmly say forgiveness does not have to mean reconciliation. Forgiveness means setting yourself free.

CHAPTER TWELVE: COMING HOME - ACHIEVING REAL FORGIVENESS

We've done a lot of groundwork now, so are you there yet? Are you beginning to feel serene and peaceful? Change happens 'sometimes quickly, sometimes slowly' as they say in 12-Step Programmes.

If you're still struggling a bit, then please remember that forgiveness is a decision. But if it's one you find hard to make, then here are the solutions. It really is time now to live in the solution and not the problem.

\
Sometimes your only available
transportation is a leap of faith.

/

Margaret J. Shepherd

How to Take that Leap of Faith

It's well known that 12-Step programmes are very successful throughout the world. Alcoholics Anonymous is perhaps the most famous one but there are many other 12-Step groups such as Overeaters Anonymous, Narcotics Anonymous, Gamblers Anonymous, Debtors Anonymous, Sex and Love Anonymous, Coda (Co-Dependents Anonymous) ACA (Adult Children of Alcoholics) where people find recovery following a 12-step programme.

All these recovering addicts are not using willpower. Instead, they have admitted they are powerless over their problem and they have turned it over to their Higher Power – whatever that may be.

These 12-Step programmes are spiritual, NOT religious. Members of these fellowships include people of all kinds of persuasion as well as agnostics and atheists.

(Personally, I believe in God, but for those who don't, just an acknowledgement that there is something greater than yourself is enough to move mountains.)

Even the cynics among us must be pretty arrogant if they think they are the greatest things on this planet! By turning their will over to their Higher Power (HP), many of these happy customers have made a settled decision. But even if they are still feeling ambivalent, the willingness to try and believe there is something more powerful than you *can* and *does* achieve miracles.

A Higher Power can be anything you choose. It could be nature, the Universe, the power of a group, your higher self, your better self. I know one man who chose Tina Turner as his Higher Power! If you're not prepared to even consider the possibility of a Higher Power, then all you need to begin to find forgiveness is a willingness to believe you don't know everything!

By turning your will over to an HP, your lower self is getting out of your own way! You will stop obsessing and ruminating in the ways you may have come to do habitually. You are dropping your arrogant characteristics by admitting the world does not revolve around you. You are acknowledging that – at some level – we are all connected. You are learning to trust in something greater than you.

I once likened my Higher Power to the workings of a satnav. When I got my first GPS system, I just loved exploring the countryside in my car. I could go up hill and down dale, pick any road that looked interesting, and explore to my heart's content. I had no fear of getting lost because I knew my satnav would get me home. For me, that's the same with God. I am free to choose my direction, but I can always be guided back on the right road if I take a wrong turn, and ask to be shown the way forward.

Self-Hypnosis

Self-hypnosis is another way of clearing away all the self-sabotaging, self-doubting aspects of our thinking. 'I want to, but I've failed in the past,' and 'I know I ought to, but I haven't got the willpower.' This is stinking thinking – hopeless for our self-esteem and made even worse when we beat ourselves up about it.

But by simply allowing our thoughts to circulate around a subject long enough, we can reach that settled decision that makes such a difference. And self-hypnosis is a way of shortcutting that process.

To produce it deliberately is no more complicated than lying still in a comfortable position and relaxing. Then think your way up through your body from your feet, through all the different areas and joints and muscles of your body, to your head. Focus on the simple sensations that we are all aware of which are often screened from everyday conscious thought. Such as the faint sensation of tingling that we all feel in the soles of our feet and our fingertips. Not noticed it yet? You will if you think closely.

Deliberately producing a physically relaxed state alters the way our cognition – our brain function – works so that the negative aspects of our thinking are temporarily suspended. This enables us to think around particular topics or subjects that may ordinarily be accompanied by anxiety or feelings of hopelessness or depression that just make us feel like a failure. In self-hypnosis, we can reach decisions about what we really want to do, freed up from self-sabotage. In simple terms, it is very similar to daydreaming and we're all good at that!

The healing power of forgiveness may already be flooding your veins, or seeping in little by little, bit by bit. I repeat, sometimes it happens quickly, sometimes slowly. As I've said before, forgiving others came much more easily to me than forgiving myself.

And one of the reasons for that is because of deep-rooted shame. That word again, often linked with abandonment issues.

Show and Tell

I tell a bit more of my story now as an example of how a dysfunctional childhood can lead to very unwise thinking. Many children adopt unhealthy survival traits that they really need to relinquish.

There was a lot of abandonment in my childhood, which left me feeling it had to be all my fault. I must have thought I'd done wrong and clearly wasn't worthy. When both your parents leave you, what else can a small child think?

I had come to the conclusion that to be safe, I had to keep my parents safe. And, until relatively recently, at some level, I felt I had to put anyone and everyone's well-being before my own. If anything went wrong, it had to be my fault and I felt 'compulsed' to put it right! Good word that, very onomatopoeic. Sounds exactly as it feels! Of course, I couldn't always to do that... and then I couldn't forgive myself. It had become a way of life.

I barely knew my Dad, even after living with him for a year, but I loved him and I loved my mum passionately. When my mother and I were reunited – after that year apart – it was bliss to be home again. But, shortly afterwards, aged just seven, I went off to a weekly boarding school, a convent, even though we weren't Catholics. I was dreadfully homesick, and I think I must have got some very peculiar and unhelpful messages about God while I was there.

I guess I picked up a lot more guilt, shame, and fear too. I remember being in my dormitory one evening when a nun told us we would all burn in hell if we'd told a lie. Hardly a helpful bedtime story for a bunch of little girls away from home.

Having endured many painful separations from my mum, I became obsessed with keeping her safe. I would do anything to protect her. Presumably, I thought if she was safe, then I'd be safe. I didn't tell her how unhappy and homesick I was at boarding school because I didn't want to hurt her. I knew my school uniform had been very expensive and money was always a problem for us. One Friday, though, after returning home alone on the Greenline bus for the weekend, I felt desperate enough to tell a grown-up friend of the family how much I missed my mum when I was away. 'You're not to tell her!' he instructed very firmly. I did as I was told.

Years later, I asked mum why she had sent me to the convent. She looked completely bewildered. 'But you wanted to go darling!' she exclaimed. Oh, so that makes it all right then? Err mum, I don't think it's wise to give a seven-year-old that decision…

I had wanted to go to boarding school, that's true. My head was full of Enid Blyton books – I couldn't get enough of Claudine at St Clare's and Malory Towers. Maybe, at some unconscious level, I thought going to boarding school would give me a break from my split loyalties towards my parents. I was obsessed with not hurting either of them. I also became obsessed with not hurting God. With not hurting anyone!

The idea of a hurt face, or a sad face, sent me into a paroxysm of sheer pain and guilt.

Most children of dysfunctional families grow up with some damaging core beliefs that need to be blown up and dispelled. They were survival mechanisms we adopted at the time that serve no function whatsoever anymore. While they're still active, though, they can make it very difficult to forgive ourselves.

I would love to see television programmes about emotional and psychological family trees! Generations of family histories charting how good and not-so-good characteristics have been handed down.

We've all made mistakes – we wouldn't be human if we hadn't. But once we've learned from them, it's time to forgive ourselves; try not to repeat them – and let them go.

> Let today be the day you stop being haunted by the ghost of yesterday. Holding a grudge & harboring anger/resentment is poison to the soul. Get even with people... but not those who have hurt us, forget them, instead get even with those who have helped us.
>
> **Steve Maraboli**
> **Author of Life, the Truth, and Being Free**

If you believe in the power of love, kindness, and compassion and have a willingness to learn, you can find forgiveness.

Task 24: Positive Changes

List your positive changes in your thinking, regarding forgiveness. Look at how far you've come and then list any remaining struggles.

It really is time to move forward now.

15 min

There is no freedom like the freedom of forgiveness. Belinda found it through her Higher Power, which was nature.

'I couldn't fully grasp the idea of God to begin with, so I chose nature as my HP. It served me very well,' she says.

'I had struggled for years to forgive my mother who was abusive and totally self-centred. I realise now she was very narcissistic and a complete control freak. When I broke up with my fiancé, four years ago, I was a complete mess and decided to sign up for therapy.'

Belinda's 'presenting problem' (as it is known) was the break-up and how to deal with it, but – of course – it wasn't long before older and deeper issues came up.

'It was a real eye-opener for me,' says Belinda. 'It made sense of so much. I realised that I'd been 'engaged' to my mother! My fiancé was also very narcissistic...'

Two years of therapy made a huge difference to Belinda's sense of well-being but she still struggled to forgive her mother and her ex-fiancé.

'I'd worked on it in therapy and had realised my mother and my ex were the products of their own dysfunctional childhoods – I actually found compassion for them both. But something in me still couldn't let go of the hurt and the resentments.'

Belinda turned to nature – her HP – for guidance and then something shifted.

'I got good messages every day from being in nature – the seasons alone tell us so much. I became more and more aware of the hope and beauty around me and bit by bit my anger, hurt, and resentment disappeared. Then one day – one night to be precise – I looked up at the stars and really got some perspective. Suddenly, I was able to forgive and let go. To do otherwise seemed ridiculous.'

Belinda's story shows how her forgiveness process unfolded over time. It also shows her willingness to put the action in. For some people, letting go happens quickly, for others slowly. For many, it's a combination of both.

When I come to letting big things go, I have a picture in my mind of a freezer defrosting. Little by little, unwanted stuff melts away. Not much seems to be happening to begin with but you've set the process in motion and a lot of work is going on behind the scenes. Then, it really gathers momentum and big chunks of the unwanted stuff fall away with a lot more ease and speed.

Time to defrost

Also, I will never forget my mum's analogy of a bag of flour for getting over heartbreak. Crying over an unfaithful boyfriend when I was 19, she said to think of the hurt as a bag of flour with a hole in it. Bit by bit the pain seeps out, and suddenly the bag is empty and feels very light. It helped at the time!

CHAPTER THIRTEEN:
SELF-ACCEPTANCE

One of the biggest, but most valuable, challenges we face in life is the art of accepting ourselves exactly as we are. The line from that famous Billy Joel song 'I love you just the way you are' is one that's melted many of us when we've heard it. It's what we all long to hear. It's what we all want, what we all need. It's what we have to do for ourselves...

If you're an atheist you might want to skip the rest of this chapter, then again you might be curious. It's entirely up to you of course but do take note of Step 2, which is: 'Came to believe that a power greater than ourselves could restore us to sanity.' So 'came to believe' means you don't have to believe right now to work the steps! *If you're uncomfortable with the God word, then simply substitute it for your Higher Power, the universe, your higher self, or your wiser self. Or Love, of course.*

Now for some very powerful information. You don't have to wait until you feel forgiveness for someone – or yourself – to forgive. As I've mentioned before, put in the action of forgiveness... and the feeling will catch up. ACCEPT AND LOVE YOURSELF JUST THE WAY YOU ARE.

Forgiveness is a choice, a decision you can make which can only benefit you and everyone in your life. Including all the people you haven't met yet! There is absolutely no downside to it.

If you feel you don't deserve to forgive yourself, then bear in mind that self-forgiveness is one of the most unselfish things you can do. Beating yourself up requires a lot of energy that is nothing other than a complete waste of time for you and everyone around you.

When I struggle to forgive myself, I need only look to the fact that struggling with it can only be a negative feeling or a negative decision. I have a strong faith, which has got deeper and deeper over the past five years.

If the God word puts you off, then substitute the word Love. And we all know that Love changes everything!

(By the way, I often work my 45-minute rule (more of that later) and my alarm went off when I finished the last sentence. It will be a good place to pick up when I come back to it!)

I was right – Love is a very good place to come back to. If we were to do everything with Love in mind, we would all be a lot healthier and happier.

As it says in Isaiah, God (or Love if you prefer) makes us as clean as freshly fallen snow. Forgiveness is a gift and we must grasp it with both hands. It is self-centred to deprive ourselves of it. Who are we to reject it? Who are we to go round and round in circles, spending time self-flagellating when we could put that energy to infinitely better use? So if you haven't already, make the decision to FORGIVE YOURSELF RIGHT NOW. Of course, you may not feel you need to do that. I say this because God, or the power of Love, forgives us regardless of whether or not we forgive ourselves.

As Iyanla Vanzant suggests in her book, *Until Today*, we should say the following: 'I am now willing to forgive myself for holding myself hostage to things God has forgiven me for.'

If you have been prone to black and white thinking – which many people who obsess about getting things right do – then I urge you now to stop doing that and think of all the shades in-between, including all the colours of the rainbow.

Whether it's forgiving others, or forgiving yourself, once you have the courage to make that decision you will know a wonderful new freedom. You will feel so much lighter when you cease to carry that huge weight on your shoulders and all that baggage that trails behind you. You will be freed from so much pain, ill health, and potential illness.

'Aah, BUT!' you might be saying, eager to look for excuses not to commit to it. Well as someone once said to me, the word BUT is always followed by b*****ks! So reframe that 'but' and think again.

Instead, think of an old-fashioned one-arm bandit machine – a fruit machine – and imagine yourself desperately trying to get all the cherries lined up in a row. This is trying to get every bit of you to agree that forgiveness of self or others is absolutely the only way forward. The odds are stacked against you managing this before you even start and so you're very unlikely to win the jackpot this way. Nonetheless, that's what I'd been trying to do. I hadn't taken into account how easy it is to argue with ourselves!

No gambling!

What I realised, not long ago, is that I had been trying to get all the metaphorical cherries in a row before I could forgive myself. In my mind, I had to magically *feel* self-forgiveness before I could allow myself to do it. I tried and tried for decades and even if I occasionally got all the cherries in a row for a second, they would very quickly get jumbled up again. Getting them still didn't make me a winner in the forgiveness stakes.

You know what? My breakthrough only appeared in a therapeutic capacity. In explaining the cherries to a client, I got it for myself. Nowadays everything doesn't have to be crystal clear before I make a decision. And, believe me, that sure frees you up to learn more and more. We have to be able to live with uncertainty because – like it or not – it's a fact of life. Life is rarely black and white; flexibility is a sign of good mental health.

Task 25: Accept Yourself Now!

15 min

Make the healthy choice NOW to accept yourself exactly the way you are. Do that, and you have instant peace. I've just up with an acronym for ACCEPT – All Creatures Could Expect Peace Today!

If you decide to think you can, then you can.

The choice is yours. Please spend 15 minutes, now, writing down your commitment to accepting yourself just the way you are. If you've time to spare, invent some acronyms for ACCEPT and PEACE which will really speak to you. To get you started, here's one for PEACE – Please Enjoy All Caring Experiences!

Across the years, I've had quite a few powerful spiritual experiences. Sometimes they've happened in very tough situations when I've been feeling quite desperate. Suddenly all the fear falls away, and I feel in total harmony with the God of my understanding.

Paul Tillich, an influential existentialist philosopher, and theologian of the 20th century, said:

> Grace strikes us when we are in great pain.
> Sometimes at that moment, a wave of light breaks
> into our darkness, and it is as though a voice were
> saying 'You are accepted'.
>
> **Paul Tillich**

Psychologist Abraham Maslow discovered in the 1960s that many healthy people reported these exquisite spiritual experiences where all fear and separation disappeared. They felt the sensation of becoming at one with the Universe, or their Higher Power. He also noted that these experiences rarely had anything to do with religion.

'Religious' is a word I feel rather uncomfortable with, because of all the negative connotations. If someone asks me if I'm religious, I tend to explain that I have faith, but religious isn't a word I use to describe it.

For all the atheists and agnostics out there, remember all you need is a mustard seed of faith in your Higher Power (whatever that may be) for things to start happening!

This reminds me of something I heard years ago that I mentioned during the TEDx talk I was asked to do in May 2017. 'God moves mountains but he expects us to have a shovel in our hands.' I suggested their shovel could be working my 15-Minute Rule!

Another terrific quote is from someone who was doing a workshop exercise in describing their journey, recently.

I am just as I am; and as I become, I am.

Workshop Attendee

Forgiveness and Acceptance go hand in hand when you think about it.

If you can accept yourself exactly the way you are, knowing you did what you did, or thought what you thought, or felt as you felt at the time, that you didn't know better, then you can make the decision to accept yourself exactly the way you are today. We are human beings and we can never be perfect. If we could have done, thought or felt differently back then we would have had more options.

If you can accept others exactly the way they are, and indeed forgive them, you will be much happier. This certainly doesn't mean you have to condone their behaviour, or reconcile with people who have hurt you or who simply are not good for you,

It's not what happens to you, but how you react to it that matters.

Epictetus

What we choose to become ideally should come from healthy choices.

Love, forgiveness, faith, gratitude, and willingness are good places from which to make positive powerful decisions.

Guilt, fear, resentment, bitterness, and self-loathing are unhelpful places – and they're not going to be part of your positive future if you so choose. They are redundant now.

The courage to be is the courage to accept oneself, in spite of being unacceptable.

Paul Tillich

Personally, I would change the 'being' of Paul's quote to 'feeling' unacceptable, and maybe that's what he meant! Read and digest more of his thinking.

\ You are accepted. You are accepted, accepted by /
that which is greater than you, and the name of
which you do not know. Do not ask for the name
now; perhaps you will find it later. Do not try to do
anything now; perhaps later you will do much. Do
not seek for anything; do not perform anything; do
not intend anything. Simply accept the fact that you
are accepted!

Paul Tillich

Completing Our Jigsaw

The road to self-acceptance, and indeed forgiveness, needs to include all the different aspects of ourselves. The good, the bad, the ugly. We need to integrate the parts we have found unacceptable until now.

We can easily 'split off' things we don't like about ourselves, and indeed do the same with regards to other people. As I've said earlier, nobody is all good or all bad. We have our qualities, we have our faults. We can never be perfect because we're human beings.

\ Until you make the unconscious conscious, it will /
direct your life and you will call it fate.

Carl Jung

Jungian psychology is very much about exploring and integrating our shadow side; the dark parts of ourselves we haven't been too keen to look at. If you find the courage to look at them, you will free yourself from so much damaging thinking.

Please choose, right now, to stop holding yourself hostage and accept yourself just the way you are. Then start loving yourself, just the way you are.

Every piece has its place

CHAPTER FOURTEEN: THE EMOTIONAL GARDENER

Let's look at this forgiveness work another way. Let's use a gardening analogy for your toolkit. (Bear with me.)

I had a chat with a young man the other day who was really worried that he might shortly do something very unwise. 'I understand what you're saying but you don't have to do that, of course,' I said. 'But the seed is planted in my head!' he said urgently. 'But you don't have to water it!' I said quickly. I'm not sure where that reply came from, exactly, but it was advice I immediately decided to start taking myself...

Nourish the good

Thinking further, and expanding on this idea, I've come to the conclusion that we would really benefit if we started work on our emotional gardening! We need to feed and water the good stuff, weed out the rubbish, and cut out the bindweed before it grows and takes hold. Then with our ground all beautifully prepared, we can start planting, nourishing, and growing. This analogy really works... so watch out world - we're getting ready to truly blossom!

Weeding

All those unhealthy weeds, such as our unhelpful habits, will be much better pulled out of our garden. Some flowers look like weeds, while other weeds look dangerously pretty and can easily be mistaken for flowers, so we need to be attentive and make wise choices. For example, I had a friend who would judge a would-be suitor by his shoes. If she didn't like them, it would be a blanket no. Not the best way to sort the wheat from the chaff. Conversely, she would fall for the guys who were into designer gear and frequented trendy restaurants. Nine times out of ten, their value systems left something to be desired. We can always ask for advice here if we're unsure whether we're looking at a flower or a weed.

When new weeds sprout, it's best to tackle them as soon as possible before they get too embedded. Speaking personally, I tackled the alcohol weed and it has been completely out of my life for a few years now. My garden is so much better without it. I replaced it with diet cola but now I've pulled that weed out too. A bottle a night of the gut-rotting stuff had become a normal part of life and that is not good for my garden!

Giving up alcohol means, among other things, that I have a lot less to *forgive myself* for these days! No more mourning after the night before, terrified that I might have done or said the wrong thing if I'd had one, or several, too many vinos.

Bindweed

Many of us have had, or have, bindweed in our garden - a big problem that's probably been around for a long time. We need to cut it right out because it's unhealthy stuff that spreads quickly and can choke or smother healthy plants.

Bindweed, just like old patterns of destructive thinking, is not easy to remove and is able to regenerate from the smallest sections. If we choose to get rid of it, then we can. I'm now working on my old habit of blaming myself for everything when something goes wrong. This bindweed has been with me since I was a small child and it's got in the way of healthy growth. It's nearly disappeared now but I know I have to be diligent until I'm confident it's gone.

Nurture

Time now to be grateful and nurture all that is healthy in our garden; this, of course, all needs regular maintenance. There is so much good in our garden that we can build on, some of which is there naturally, and some of which we've put in with our own fair hands. Those seeds were fed and watered, and now we're enjoying the fruits of our labour. At times, we've been offered help and – at other times – we've actively sought it. There is much expertise to choose from.

Our inner resources have also come to the rescue when the landscape has been threatened by stormy conditions. Then, when the weather is calm and sunny again, our garden looks better than ever. Personally, having survived four severe storms that arrived together back in 2012 – all of which uprooted so much – I'm enjoying my maturing garden more than ever before!

Planting

With our emotional garden benefitting from the love and care we are now giving it, we can delight in choosing what else to plant. Which seeds do we really want to cultivate? Imagine our absolute joy when we see them grow and blossom. If we pick our ideas well, we're in for a fabulous view! Here I think it would be a good idea for us to visualise how we want our garden to be – how it should look, smell, feel, and what it should evoke. Then we need to write it down because (statistically) we're much more likely to achieve our goal if we do that. Once we're ready to plant, we can then hand it over and trust in a power greater than ourselves to do the rest.

Happy planting!

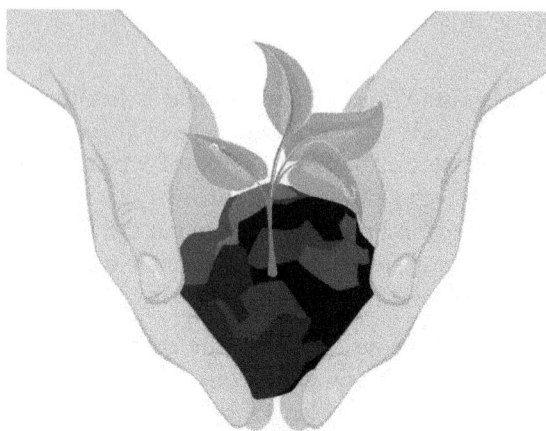

Gently does it

Patience

Some plants take longer to show results than others. Some wither and die because we didn't nurture them enough, some give up despite all our care; others blossom beautifully even if we haven't given them as much attention as they might deserve. If we've done our bit, and put the work in, the rest is out of our hands.

A lot of us will admit to feeling frustrated when we don't receive instant gratification. (We might even be tempted to abandon all, and rush to the shops for a bouquet of picked flowers that will last all of five days if we're lucky.) Much worse, though, is when nothing seems to be happening despite us putting so much effort in. This is when we're in real danger of giving up. We need to choose to develop patience here and keep on nurturing things. Patience is a key tool for any gardener.

I'm using this (patience) on my current attempt to lose weight. When I jump on the scales with excitement, expecting to have lost a couple of pounds only to find I've gained weight, I could scream! 'It's not fair!' I shriek inwardly. 'I've done everything I'm supposed to!' In the past, I would have pressed the 'F*** it' button at this point and abandoned the diet.

Last month when the scales betrayed my efforts again, I chose to do something different. I turned away from the 'F*** it' button and instead planted the seed to carry on being as good as gold and trust

84

that all would be well. Guess what? Next time I got on the scales I'd lost a couple of pounds! At the time of writing, I've just had another weigh in – and it's not showing the result I want. Yet. Through gritted teeth, I am reminding myself not to give up and be patient! Evidence has already shown me that patience works.

There will always be something to work on in the garden – we need to think *progress*, not perfection.

Obviously, while tending our gardens, we need to work with the seasons – and circumstances beyond our control – but that's a doddle if we choose to learn the art of acceptance. 'This too will pass' is a good phrase to remember. Spring will always follow winter, no matter how hard the ground has been.

> There are things in my life that are hard to reconcile, like divorce. Sometimes it is very difficult to make sense of how it could possibly happen. Laying blame is so easy. I don't have time for hate or negativity in my life. There's no room for it.
>
> **Reese Witherspoon**

CHAPTER FIFTEEN: A FULL HOUSE OF ACE CARDS!

In my first 15-Minute Rule book, I introduced my ACE card. This is an acronym I came up with for *Attitude Changes Everything.*

ACE: Attitude Changes Everything

Attitude sure does change everything. My other big mantra, as I have already mentioned, is Choose Your Thoughts Wisely because how we think is how we feel.

Look at your attitude to some of your troubling thoughts and see if you need to change it. We don't want to be a slave to our destructive and unhelpful thoughts in any way. We want to embrace and follow the good ones.

So think about that Ace card and how it is up your sleeve all the time. It can always turn a negative into a positive. Immediately, if you choose. The way we choose to perceive something will influence how we deal with it.

Positive Mental Attitude is a phrase that has been around for donkeys' years, and for very good reason. It works if you work it. Let's use it on a forgiveness issue shall we?

Scenario: Jane cannot forgive her boyfriend Paul for lying about the fact he had spent two years in prison for fraud. They had been seeing each other for a year before she found out. She ended the relationship just as he was about to move in with her. Paul has begged for her forgiveness, but she says she can never trust him again.

Paul is devastated and explained to Jane that he didn't dare tell her about his time in prison because he thought she would drop him instantly. He is deeply remorseful for his crime, and extremely sorry that he kept the truth from her.

Jane chose to ditch Paul immediately because she felt it was the right thing to do. She can't forgive him for the deceit. However, she misses him very much and had felt sure they had a future together. She feels bereft, cheated, silly, and humiliated.

At this point, Jane could pull out her Ace card from up her sleeve and look at it another way.

If she forgives him, she would feel better very quickly. This doesn't mean she has to get together with him again (although, of course, she does have a choice in the matter). If they did reconcile, they would obviously need to work on trust issues if their relationship was worth saving. If she chooses not to go back with him, she will have learned from the experience, which can only stand her in good stead for her next relationship.

Jane might also be angry with herself for putting her trust in Paul and for being 'conned' by him. Again, if she gets her Ace card out, she can choose to forgive herself and move on. There is a big guarantee here. If Jane uses her Ace card for forgiveness, she will undoubtedly feel peaceful. She will stop castigating herself very quickly.

She could also add to this an attitude of gratitude, because that always changes everything. Appreciation or gratitude boosts our well-being no end. When we're feeling appreciative or grateful for all the good things in our life, it cannot help but lift our spirits. Beyond that, we can be appreciative and grateful for the difficult things too. Because we can learn from them, if we choose to, and definitely become stronger as a result.

Now for some more exciting news. We all have a full house of Ace cards at our disposal. Awareness of them can change everything for the better! So let Awareness be the next one in the set.

ACE: Awareness Changes Everything

Awareness, awareness, awareness! So very important. The more awareness we have, the more we learn; the more we learn, the more awareness we have. Another win-win situation then. To clarify the meaning of awareness, the Oxford dictionary definition says it is knowledge or perception of a situation or fact.

Awareness is obviously very helpful in every aspect of life. Being aware when you're in the moment or looking at the past and the future with awareness can only be beneficial. Using it around Forgiveness can only be a very good thing.

Back to Jane, our scenario example. Here are some ways her Ace card of Awareness could really help her.

In the moment: while she's actively feeling she can't forgive Paul, she could use her Awareness card to consciously accept those feelings.

In the past: She could decide to become aware of what in the past has led her to believe she cannot forgive Paul. She could then question those beliefs and challenge them.

In the future: Does she want to carry on the rest of her life with her black and white take on forgiveness? She could use her Awareness card to actively choose her best way forward. Awareness gives her the choice.

ACE: Acceptance Changes Everything

Another vital Ace card we all have up our sleeve. Years ago I had a message from my Higher Power to accept everything with love.

It was – and is – a fabulous message, and despite writing myself shorthand reminder notes to AWL (Accept With Love), I often forgot to do just that. When I do though, what a difference it makes to my well-being.

I am trying to do it more regularly now, because once the message drops from my head to my heart, I feel so much better. Calmer, relieved, at peace, in harmony.

Like Forgiveness, Acceptance does not mean we have to condone unacceptable behaviour.

How could acceptance help our character Jane? She could choose to accept how upset she was by Paul's lie; she could accept that she doesn't know whether or not she could trust him again; she could accept that she needs time to process the experience before she makes a decision about whether or not to reconcile; she could accept that she can forgive him – and herself – regardless of whether or not she goes back to him.

ACE: Action Changes Everything

This is your fourth ace and what a winner! The 15-Minute Rule is geared up to Action. Positive action cannot fail to bring positive results. You can solve any problem with the 15-Minute Rule, believe me. By using it, you have stopped procrastinating and are taking action.

> Our main business is not to see what lies dimly at a
> distance, but to do what lies clearly at hand.

Thomas Carlyle

Back to our friend Jane: If she decides to use her Action card she will save herself many hours of procrastination and spare herself the torture of her head going round and round the same old circles and still not knowing what to do for the best. If she takes action, sets her timer for 15 minutes, and brainstorms what she should do about it in her safe time frame, she will be well on her way to a solution. When she eventually makes her decision she can relax in the knowledge that she's going to know some peace and serenity. Even if it later proves to be the wrong decision, she did her best and she will know that it felt right at the time.

Taking action with forgiveness really will change your life for the better.

Remember all you need to do to start is set your timer for 15 minutes and start brainstorming on how you're going to conquer this mountain.

> The moment one definitely commits oneself,
> then providence moves too. All sorts of things
> occur to help one that would never otherwise
> have occurred.

Goethe

So there you have your full house of Ace cards: Attitude, Awareness, Acceptance and Action. A very powerful hand.

Task 26 Playing Your Hand

15 min

Write down how you will use your full house to help any remaining forgiveness issues.

NB: If each and every one of us took care of our own small corner – in terms of forgiveness – we really would have world peace!

There are dark shadows on the earth, but its lights are stronger in the contrast.

Charles Dickens

CHAPTER SIXTEEN: ORGANISE DON'T AGONISE

If you haven't yet grasped the importance and life-enhancing notion of forgiveness by now, then herewith some extras for your toolkit.

> Forgiveness goes beyond human fairness: it is pardoning those things that can't readily be pardoned at all.
>
> **C.S. Lewis**

Sweet, Sweet Music

Music, as we know, is a fantastic way of getting in touch with our emotions. It often hits the spot immediately and/or reaches the parts that might otherwise be suppressed.

Straight to the soul

Here is some suggested listening around the topic of Forgiveness. Use Google or YouTube to locate them and explore music generally with forgiveness in mind.

- Less Than Whole by Eric Paslay
- Forgiveness (Lyrics) by Matthew West
- Fall Into Me by Jamie Lawson
- Tell Your Heart To Beat Again (Lyrics) by Danny Gokey
- Forgiveness by Sam Feldt, feat Joe Cleere
- Forgiveness and Love by Miley Cyrus
- I Was Wrong by Robin Schulz
- Miracle of Love by Jamie Lawson
- Love One Another by Luacine Clark Fox
- Sorry by Caroline and Colin or Justin Bieber
- Everybody Hurts by REM
- Bring You Home by Ronan Keating
- 'I believe' by Frankie Laine
- 'Things I Thought I'd Never Do' by Jack Savoretti
- 'Amazing Grace' by John Newton
- 'Before the throne of God above' by Charitie Lees Bancroft
- You Say by Lauren Daigle
- Redemption Song by Bob Marley
- I Shall Be Released by Bob Dylan
- A Little Mercy by Jamie Lawson
- Good Good Father by Chris Tomlin

Ho'oponopono

Ho'oponopono is an ancient Hawaiian practice of forgiveness. The mantra is: I am sorry, please forgive me, thank you, I love you.

Across all cultures, these words have great value. There can't be many people in the world who wouldn't like to be able to say them, or to hear them. It is something we all have in common and, to me, is evidence of our connection with the true essence of each other and ourselves.

Basically, the idea of ho'oponopono is that it removes all negative beliefs that may have been holding us back. By practicing the simple steps of Repentance, Forgiveness, Gratitude and Love, we will be able to release so much unhealthy baggage. The practice will cleanse our sub-conscious and we can feel whole again. Painful memories can be replaced with love. What's more, the willingness to forgive and love will touch everyone in the universe if we choose to believe we are all united.

Ho'oponopono, in common with other shamanic traditions, teaches us that we are all connected and by practicing their four unifying concepts, we can heal ourselves and others too.

Let Go

We need to let go of any attachment to unforgiveness.

If you're finding it difficult, then ask yourself what the pay-off is. Believe me, there will be one!

A bit of a facer, this next question, but perhaps you need to ask yourself whether you're addicted to suffering? Perhaps you are so habitually attached to it that the release from it feels too scary. After all, it would mean looking squarely at that frightening word 'CHANGE'!

Well, you know what they say, change is as good as a rest and all that. Moving out of your comfort zone, however alien and unpleasant that feels, is necessary here. Once you've jumped that hurdle, you will soon see how fabulously rewarding constructive change is.

So how do you move out of that comfort zone? By acknowledging that if you're choosing to think, and therefore to feel differently, it will seem very strange to begin with. Even if it's doing you the world of good! Think of it as trying on a new pair of shoes. No matter how much you like them, or how useful they will be, they will feel very odd to begin with. They will not feel comfy like your old ones! Until you get used to wearing them, that is.

What You Resist, Persists

I urge you to look at the feeling that is behind any remaining resistance to forgiveness. And then let that go!

But, can you move on *without* forgiveness? The answer to that has to be of course you can move on without forgiveness (holding on to the opinions, assessments and experiences that have got you to where you are today). But life needs to be about evolving and hopefully improving yourself; if you cannot forgive, you will be severely hampering the process. It would like running a marathon carrying a ton of needless extra weight. Why would you want to do that?

Do not follow where the path may lead. Go, instead, where there is no path and leave a trail…

Ralph Waldo Emerson

Task 27: I's

15 min

A therapist friend of mine once drew me a picture of the following. It was a block capital I, filled with lots of little lower case i(s).

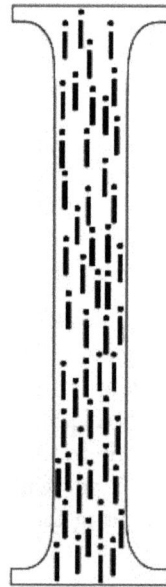

Please use the 15-Minute Rule to draw yourself the same picture!

My friend pointed out the big I is us, and the little i(s) are all our different characteristics, both good and not so good. When we're upset about something, we can have a tendency to focus on that one particular thing and give it far too much weight. For example, we may be thinking we're just not good enough to find new love.

Here's where we need to look at other i(s) that tell us to stop talking rubbish and look at the facts that tell us we most certainly are good enough!

Name the I's

Now taking things one step further, I would like you to name all your little i's. For example, Addictive Annie, Compulsive Charlie, Kind

Kim, Loving Luke, Nurturing Nellie, Negative Norman, Positive Peter, etc.

Then when Worrying Wendy or Obsessive Ollie starts giving you the washing machine head, you can invite Calming Chloe or Parent Paul in, to give you some perspective.

Task 28: Rock and Screen

15 min This exercise is very good for those times when thoughts or images keep going round and round in your head. My friend, author Sandra Sedgbeer, told me it was something she learned when she was studying NLP.

She says: 'Find a quiet place. Bring the story, thought or picture to mind, visualize it playing out like something you're watching on a television screen... see the story, thought or sequence unfolding in front of you and imagine that you have a big rock in your hand.

'Throw the rock at the imaginary screen, watch the screen crack and then shatter into dozens of pieces that fall to the ground, leaving you looking at an empty TV that simply starts dissolving in front of you; or you see an empty space altogether.

'This is often enough to 'break the pattern' of thought/vision.

'It's a tool for erasing a software program that our brain is running and can be used on any uncomfortable thought or vision or pattern that we need to get out of our mind and life.'

Thanks Sandie!

The Power of Three

I love the number three and I am not alone. It sounds good, solid, warm and safe. We like to think in threes – beginning, middle, end; mind, body, spirit, the Holy Trinity, ABC, and so on. When used with the 15-Minute Rule, it can inspire a positive mindset.

You can be as creative as you like with your threes. You could do three lots of 15 minutes on your forgiveness work, today; you could choose three people from your divorce that you have been struggling to forgive; you could give yourself three months to resolve every single struggle you have around the life-changing concept of forgiveness.

You can use the Power of Three in any way you choose of course – for example, three tasks, three days, three months, three different projects to have on the go; all of which would benefit from using your 15-Minute Rule.

The 45-Minute Rule

The Power of Three brings me on neatly to talk more about how the 15-Minute Rule has evolved very nicely onto my 45-Minute Rule. Three lots of 15 minutes make 45 minutes, of course! Again, it feels like a very safe and contained space. I use it as often as I use my first rule now and, naturally, I've used it to write this book. Use it when you are completely au fait with the 15-Minute Rule, and would benefit from more time on certain projects – i.e. you don't want to interrupt the flow when you've really got your teeth into something,

45 minutes works very well. You can then reward yourself with a 15-minute break!

Read and Digest

Suffering teaches us so much if we let it. It is often the springboard to tremendous growth. Hopefully, most of us know that we cannot change anyone except ourselves.

Many years ago, one of the big boys in the therapy world, Carl Jung, kindly revealed the contents of a letter he had received. He said: 'Recently I received a letter from a former patient, which describes the necessary transformation in simple but trenchant words'. She writes:

'Out of evil, much good has come to me. By keeping quiet, repressing nothing, remaining attentive, and by accepting reality - taking things as they are, and not as I wanted them to be - by doing all this, unusual knowledge has come to me, and unusual powers as well, such as I would never have imagined before. I always thought that when we accepted things they overpowered us in some way or other. This turns out not to be true at all, and it is only by accepting them that one can assume an attitude towards them. So now I intend to play the game of life, being receptive to whatever comes to me, good and bad, sun and shadow forever alternating, and, in this way, also accepting my own nature with its positive and

negative sides. Thus everything becomes more alive to me. What a fool I was! How I tried to force everything to go according to the way I thought it ought to!'

We would all benefit from taking this on board. It's powerful stuff.

Task 29: Confront Outdated Beliefs

Look at your old, outdated beliefs and challenge them.

15 min

For example, 'I can't forgive anyone who betrayed me' or 'Who am I to forgive myself? I don't deserve it.' Our beliefs are the framework upon which we build our todays and tomorrows, so it is very important to make sure our belief system is healthy. If we grew up believing we're not allowed to feel angry or we're 'not good enough' then we need to change these quickly. Of course, we're allowed to feel anger, and we're perfectly entitled to that as long as we don't act on it and harm anyone, including ourselves.

Any of your beliefs that prevent your growth are not going to be helpful to you.

Acknowledge Your Anger

You may be well aware of your anger surrounding your divorce, in which case you're right on track to start accepting it. It's ok to feel angry! The next step is to process it, with the help of a trusted friend or a therapist. Then, make plans on how you can manage and deal with it appropriately. Of course, there may be big feelings of injustice around, which is perfectly natural. Some of them could well have links to injustices from your childhood. Having said that, underneath the anger will also be great sadness. We need to acknowledge and accept that, too.

Now, let's look at anger from the point of view of people who struggle to acknowledge it. I used to be like that, but not anymore – and that's a big relief.

Let me tell you a story... This doesn't relate directly to divorce, but it could well press bells for anyone suffering with anger they haven't dared face.

I have a neighbour who was, quite frankly, a nightmare. A total nightmare. She created problems for many people who crossed her path.

I struggled to forgive her but, I am happy to say, I managed to do just that eventually. Then some time later, without her knowing it, she did me a huge favour. I was passing her one day, when all the deeply unpleasant things she had done resurfaced, and the thought crossed my mind, 'Well, I could always top myself if she gets too much.'

I was shocked and horrified with myself! What on earth was I thinking? And then I realised... I felt so angry with all the upset she had caused people, including my daughter and me, that I had shoved it down inside me because I didn't know what to do with it. Basically, I had turned that anger on myself. Once I acknowledged that I felt really angry with *her*, the suicidal thoughts evaporated instantly.

While I had already forgiven this neighbour, I realised I hadn't recognized and accepted just how angry I still was. Once I'd done that, I could let the anger go.

I then came to realise, first-hand, that when I had experienced suicidal thoughts before, they were probably all about my anger turned inwards.

I began to look back and face the suppressed anger of my past – around my divorce, people who had really hurt my daughter, people who had really hurt me, and the hugely difficult times in my childhood. It was really liberating!

Because I was not emotionally attached to the neighbour, maybe I felt safe enough to get in touch with those angry feelings?

Lots of people have suicidal thoughts from time to time. And, often, they are all about repressed or suppressed anger.

Suicidal thoughts, of course, don't mean that you're about to do away with yourself. Many of us have these thoughts from time to time when we're in awful pain. It's not that we want to kill ourselves – it's just that we want the pain to stop.

Thousands of people in the UK die by suicide each year. According to the Mental Health Foundation, it is the leading cause of death among young people between the ages of 20-34, men being three times more likely to take their own lives than women. Furthermore, it is the leading cause of death for men under 50 in the UK.

One reason why men are more likely to commit suicide is that they are less likely to ask for help than women, and also less likely to talk about such feelings. Only 27% of people who died by suicide between 2005 and 2015 had been in contact with mental health services in the year before their death. Talking about such matters is vital and necessary to prevent further suicides.

The Mental Health Foundation's recent stress survey found that 32% of adults who had felt stress at some point in their lives had experienced suicidal thoughts. Those thoughts were probably all about denying their anger. Repressing, or suppressing them, is no good for anyone.

Repressed anger is unconscious. Suppressed anger, on the other hand, is conscious; a refusal to experience the rage (probably for fear of perceived reprisals).

I am a great believer in talking about such thoughts to someone you trust because it takes a lot of anger's power away, and lightens the load. Suppressed anger is behind a lot of clinical depression and if it's acknowledged in a healthy and appropriate way, the depression will often lift.

Many children suppress their angry thoughts, especially if it's towards their loved ones. I had a lot of repressed and suppressed anger as a child and didn't dare acknowledge it until recently. Unconsciously, I had been terrified that if I went anywhere near such thoughts, I would be forever abandoned.

Children feel there is something wrong with them if they're neglected. And if they feel angry about it, they can then feel guilty. Shame takes hold, and they quickly turn the anger inwards and convince themselves they're not worth loving.

We're all worth loving, every single one of us!

Paralysis of Analysis

Overthinking can be a major problem for many of us. Thinking about things can, in fact, lead to a lack of action because all you do is think about things! If that happens, then it's all too easy to find yourself in the *paralysis of analysis*.

The answer is simple. LET GO OF THINKING! Enjoy the present. I totally agree with author and spiritual teacher Eckhart Tolle who says that thinking is an addiction many of us are in denial about. 'Becoming more aware of the present moment and accepting it as it is slows down the over-active mind.'

Of course, we need to think – but we don't need to be addictive or obsessive about it.

'Can't stop drinking, can't stop thinking, can't stop smoking, can't stop eating,' says Eckhart. 'Can't stop thinking is a drug that's been around for so long and it's a pseudo sense of self.'

He explains that most people are reluctant to let go of it because they equate not thinking with being asleep.

If we learn to stay more in the moment, instead of fretting about yesterday or worrying about tomorrow, we will become so much happier. Obsessive guilt and worrying are destructive pastimes. They achieve nothing except more angst. Once we become aware of our tendency to do this, we can let go of it much more easily.

'Thinking then loses the ability to create havoc in your life and confuse you,' says Eckhart. 'When you see it you are not completely addicted anymore. You're only completely addicted when you don't see it. When you see it, you are the awareness. When there is no awareness, you are it. And you are the ego. And you are addicted to the ego, which is addicted to unhappiness.'

Hold your HP's Hand

I came up with this one recently, and I find it very helpful. If you're feeling really anxious or unsure about something, then visualise holding your Higher Power's hand. Actually visualise it as if it were a physical, warm, solid hand.

Tension will fly out of you. You will feel your confidence growing almost immediately.

The hand of faith

Beyond Ego

If we want to wake up and smell the roses, then we need to get beyond our ego.

People think of ego as being arrogant, but that's just one part of it. Our ego is of our own construction and frequently gets in our way with its unhelpfulness. It obstructs our spiritual growth and our human potential like nothing else can. It is made up of many different beliefs we have picked up that form an untrue picture of ourselves.

We develop a concept of self as children and that old self-image – with often contradictory beliefs – needs to be left behind now we're adults.

Everyone's ego is personal to them. Difficult emotions such as anger, jealousy, resentment, and insecurity can often be tied up with our ego, our false self. We might get very angry with one part of our ego, and then beat ourselves up for that with another part.

We need to let go of these false ego beliefs, rise above them, and reach in to our loving, divine selves.

Moving On

We've all dreamed of living happily ever after...

For many of us, the story went like this: boy meets girl (or whatever combination of that is your thing), they fall blissfully in love, and then they walk off into the sunset, happily ever after.

Or, in film versions, the couple meet, they fall in love, they fall out *big time*, and then they reconcile, happily ever after...

As we now know, this is rarely the case! The good news is, we can learn some amazing lessons from these hideously painful experiences if we so choose...

Divorce might be the end of a relationship as we knew it, but it is also an opportunity to really open up a wonderful new relationship with YOURSELF. The more you understand you, the better equipped you are to find deepening and lasting happiness.

As for my own divorce, it was a major turning point. I knew it was time to really work on myself and sort out all the unresolved baggage from my family background. To do that I needed to stay single until I had done the necessary soul searching. No man – or woman – can ever 'fix' us! I decided that if ever I went into a relationship again, then I wanted to make sure I was in a position to finally pick well.

Unlike my ex-husband, who himself said that he can't be alone, I found the courage to become a person in my own right. You know something? I hate that expression 'My other half' because it is so co-dependent! As I said in my Agony columns, more than once, the best relationships are made up of two whole people, not two halves. A loving partner needs to be the icing on the cake. The cake itself, needs to be nutritious, delicious, and rise up all by itself.

It was definitely time to take my own advice...

I've been single for seven years and at long last, I feel ripe and ready for a new relationship. What's so lovely now is I don't actually need one. I'm happy without a man, which paradoxically means I'm fit for a relationship!

I'm totally relaxed about what the future holds. I've just started having the odd date, but I'm in no rush to find romantic love. Love is all around us, as the song goes, and we can find it in all sorts of relationships that don't involve sex.

What would I say to someone who wrote to me with exactly the same story as mine? I'd say 'You've come a long way, darlin' – keep up the good work!'

Visualise

Driving along in my car a little while ago, I asked myself how I would feel if I could truly forgive myself. Well, I felt instantly calm and peaceful, with a huge knowledge that it would enable me to give more than I do already. Therefore, my friends, how could it not be the right thing to do?

For further inspiration, take note of the following quotation:

> ...and then the day came when the risk to remain tight in a bud was more painful than the risk it took to blossom.
>
> **Anais Nin**

Today, I have forgiven myself. How could I not... knowing what I do today?

Can you do the same now? Can you forgive yourself for all your real and imagined wrongdoings? You *can* for sure, but WILL you? Are you going to make a healthy choice here, to do the right thing? Please do, because your life will become so much better, richer, and happier.

Can you forgive everyone in your life who has hurt you? Or, even more difficult, hurt your child? Again, you *can*, but WILL you? Your choice, of course, but you now have many more tools to help you make that good decision. What do you think your Higher Power, or your divine intelligence, or the wise part of yourself, is saying to you here?

Forgive, forgive, forgive.

So let go of negative, punishing, ego-driven thoughts; and if you ever need a reminder, simply visualise what the unforgiveness of others and yourself means to you now. Horrible, eh? Unhealthy, unloving, toxic.

Not get in touch with what total forgiveness would mean to you again. Visualise it, touch, smell, taste and hear it. Bask in the bliss because you deserve it.

Your Higher Power forgives you and loves you unconditionally. Accept that wholeheartedly and follow the example. It's the only way to travel.

With love,

Caroline xxx

OTHER BOOKS

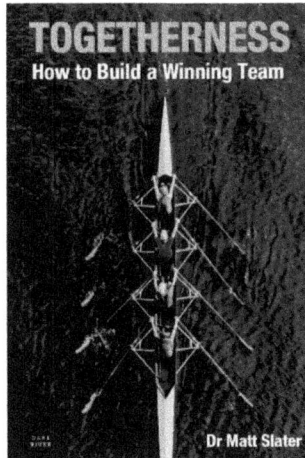

Togetherness: How to Build a Winning Team by Dr Matt Slater

Togetherness is a powerful state of connection between individuals that can lead to amazing triumphs. In sport, teams win matches, but teams with togetherness win championships and make history.

If you want the individuals on your team to develop their skills and reach their potential, get them 'together'. The key to this, is to understand your players' group memberships and how to harness them, to create a unique team identity that is special to "us".

This concise and practical book – from Dr. Matt Slater, a world authority on togetherness – shows you how you can develop togetherness in your team. The journey starts with an understanding of what underpins togetherness and how it can drive high performance and well-being simultaneously. It then moves onto practical tips and activities based on the 3R model (Reflect, Represent, Realise) that you can learn and complete with your team to unlock their togetherness.

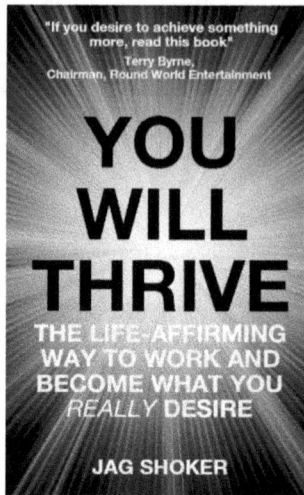

"If you desire to achieve something more, read this book"
Terry Byrne,
Chairman, Round World Entertainment

YOU WILL THRIVE

THE LIFE-AFFIRMING WAY TO WORK AND BECOME WHAT YOU *REALLY* DESIRE

JAG SHOKER

You Will Thrive: The Life-Affirming Way to Work and Become What You Really Desire by Jag Shoker

Have you lost your spark or the passion for what you do? Is your heart no longer in your work or (like so many people) are you simply disillusioned by the frantic race to get ahead in life? Your sense of unease may be getting harder to ignore, and comes from the growing urge to step off the treadmill and pursue a more thrilling *and* meaningful direction in life.

You Will Thrive addresses the subject of modern disillusionment. It is essential reading for people looking to make the most of their talents and be something more in life. Something that matters. Something that makes a difference in the world.

Through six empowering steps, it reveals 'the Way' to boldly follow your heart as it leads you to the perfect opportunities you seek. Through every step, it urges you to put a compelling thought to the test:

You possess the power within you to attract the right people, opportunities, and circumstances that you need to become what you desire.

As you'll discover, if you find the *faith* to act on this power and do the Work required to realise your dream, a testing yet life-affirming path will unfold before you as life *orchestrates* the Way to make it all happen.

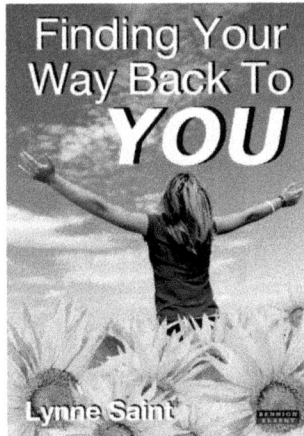

Finding Your Way Back to YOU: A self-help book for women who want to regain their Mojo and realise their dreams! By Lynne Saint.

Are you at a crossroads in life, lacking in motivation, looking for a new direction or just plain 'stuck'?

Finding your Way back to YOU is a focused and concise resource written specifically for women who have found themselves in any of the positions above.

The good news is that you already have all of the resources you need to solve your own problems; this practical book helps you remove the barriers that prevent this from happening.

Designed as a practical book with an accompanying downloadable journal and weblinked exercises, *Finding Your Way Back to YOU* is an inspiring book that introduces Neuro- Linguistic Programming, and Cognitive Behavioural Therapy techniques for change that are particularly valuable within the coaching context.

> Recognise Who and What is holding you back

> Make a commitment to yourself and your future

> Boost your self-confidence and self-esteem

> Identify and Challenge your limiting beliefs

> Regain your life balance

> Supercharge your self-image

> Get motivated… Achieve your life goals

Also available as an audiobook

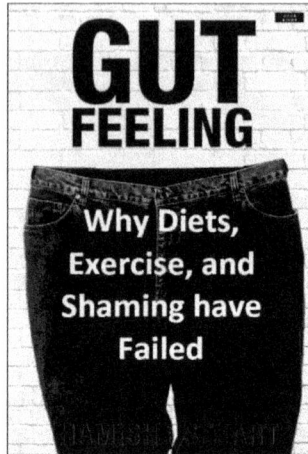

Gut Feeling: Why Diets, Exercise, and Shaming have Failed by
Hamish Stuart

There is one certainty in the obesity debate – the dominant messages
about diet, willpower, and fat-shaming have failed in the last 40 years;
in fact, things have got worse.

We need a new approach. We need to give fat people a voice.

Gut Feeling is the story of why 'traditional' approaches fail to stop
expanding waistlines – and what you can do about it.

We need to understand why 'Eat Less, Move More' has not worked,
why exercise is only part of any solution, and why fat-shaming makes
things worse. We have to do what the science is actually telling us –
what people can do, not what others think they should do.

Gut Feeling takes aim at the major players in the obesity crisis. From
the manufacturers of processed food and fizzy drinks, to the dieting
industry, to exercise gurus, to governments. The obesity debate is
starting from the wrong place, dominated by people who do not really
understand the big picture.

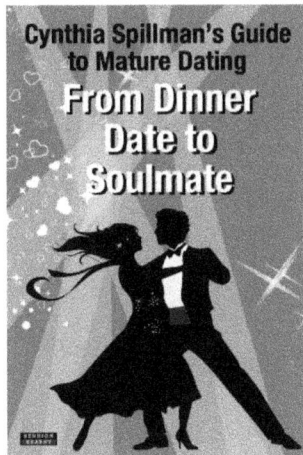

From Dinner Date to Soulmate – Cynthia Spillman's Guide to Mature Dating by Cynthia Spillman

Are you reaching a more mature stage in life and looking for a new relationship? Are you tentatively returning to the dating arena following the end of a relationship? Do you want to successfully find the man of your dreams and avoid the many pitfalls?

This book is for you.

Written by international dating coach Cynthia Spillman, founder of The International Dating Academy and formerly the Chief Executive of Dinner Dates, From Dinner Date to Soulmate is a humorous, practical, and inspirational handbook for the growing mature dating market.

Cynthia shows how searching for a fulfilling new relationship must be undertaken mindfully and strategically, and that in order to attract the partner she deserves – a woman must first feel good about herself. Cynthia guides readers through a series of proven steps, encouraging them to examine their previous relationship patterns, and provides a whole host of mature dating skills, strategies, and techniques to be put into practice.

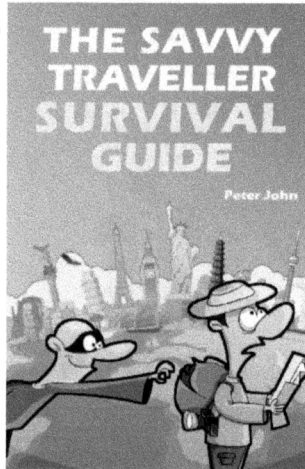

The Savvy Traveller Survival Guide by Peter John

Travel is one of our favourite activities. From the hustle of bustle of the mega-cities to sleepy mountain towns to the tranquillity and isolation of tropical islands, we love to get out there and explore the world.

But globe-trotting also comes with its pitfalls. Wherever there are travellers, there are swindlers looking to relieve individuals of their money, possessions and sometimes even more. To avoid such troubles, and to get on with enjoyable and fulfilling trips, people need to get smart. This book shows you how.

The Savvy Traveller Survival Guide offers practical advice on avoiding the scams and hoaxes that can ruin any trip. From no-menu, rigged betting, and scenic taxi tour scams to rental damage, baksheesh, and credit card deceits – this book details scam hotspots, how the scams play out and what you can do to prevent them. The Savvy Traveller Survival Guide will help you develop an awareness and vigilance for high-risk people, activities, and environments.

Forewarned is forearmed!